Inconsequential
Child

Overcoming Emotional Neglect

One man's journey to love and hope through
mindfulness and individuation

Anthony Martino

The Inconsequential Child

Overcoming Emotional Neglect

Published in the United States of America by Vangelo Media; www.vangelomedia.com. Send inquiries to info@vangelomedia.com.

Publisher's Cataloging-in-Publication data

Martino, Anthony.

The Inconsequential Child : Overcoming Childhood Emotional Neglect / Anthony Martino.

ISBN: 978-0-9886791-7-7

Summary: A personal journey toward emotional well-being, love and hope through the pursuit of Jungian individuation. An autobiographical account of mindfulness and psychotherapy described from past experiences and real-time self-analysis as the author overcomes his childhood emotional neglect.

Vignettes

earliest memory.....3

a letter and a request.....4

memories.....8

learnings.....10

inadvertent effects.....13

ignore not, force not.....16

first step.....20

harmful protection and truthful lie.....25

find yourself by letting go.....30

obvious, yet invisible.....32

overwhelming boxes.....36

recursive identity.....42

observing everything, yet seeing nothing.....45

cognizant unconsciousness.....50

feel not.....53

oblivious avoidance.....55

stifled emotions.....58

family tenet.....62

painful joy.....65

my mother's son.....67

ignored needs.....70

finding connections.....72

emotional intellect.....76

fearless heart.....79

noonies.....84

fear-less-hope-less-fear.....91

a framework.....94

self-love empowers connectedness.....98

relationships through vulnerability.....102

essence masking.....104

truth from any angle.....106

mindful choice.....110

additive moments.....115

finding your stranger.....117

discover your essence.....122

faith & love, serenity & grace.....125

earliest memory

It is dark, very dark.

The dull light from another room painted half of her body as she stood there yelling at him.

No light illuminates him as he responds in kind.

I am huddled in a corner; leaning on a step.

She was in her nightgown. He was in his underwear.

They are tall and very far away.

I reached out and touched the back of his leg. He picked me up and held me in his big arms.

She yelled some more.

He put me down.

In the dark.

Unseen.

Unheard.

a letter and a request

Dear Reader,

Please allow me to open my heart to you in the form of a letter. I will talk openly about my failings, fears, and foibles. As I share my life with you, I hope you will see them as I now do, beautiful artifacts of me. If, in the process of reading this letter, you learn of your imperfections, I ask that you acknowledge them and hold them to your heart with open honesty. Hopefully, you will accept them as beautiful artifacts of you.

A few years ago, the notion of writing a letter to a stranger, would have never entered my mind. You see, I avoided people whenever possible. They drained me. Today, however, I welcome interactions of any kind with everyone. I am a changed man. I have been on a journey and found something I need to share with others.

My journey began a half dozen years ago when I realized I had an inconsequential child hiding within me. I did not know why or how that child got there; only that he was there huddled in the dark. At that time, I was focused only on one thing, to find that child. Along the way however, I realized that I was also living a life devoid of emotion. A realization that both stunned me and confused me. I was now on a journey to find that child and also my emotions. Eventually, I found a treasure that has not only changed my relationships with people, it has also changed the relationship I have with myself.

I am writing this letter because I want you to have that treasure too. The treasure I have found is limitless, pervasive and unique to me. If you are lucky enough to

4

find the treasure, it will be uniquely yours. I want you to have the treasure because its value to me will increase when you find it, and we can be in relationship together, without fear. There is no need for you to hurry and find the treasure because it is not possible to find it until you are capable of seeing it. I am certain, however, that you will find the treasure. It will be there, waiting for you, and only for you, when you are ready to pursue your journey.

Later, after I have fully described the treasure, I will rewrite the previous paragraph and replace the words 'treasure' and 'it' with the actual treasure. I am certain, the rewritten paragraph will be more understandable and enlightening. For now, I only ask that you allow me to share my journey with you so that I can describe the treasure I have found and you can benefit from its riches.

This book is an intimate memoir of my journey from a dull, emotionless life to hope and love. I am sharing my journey with you so that you will come to believe that love and hope are not only possible but intrinsic to your being. I want you to benefit from my learnings, so your life and the lives of those around you are more fulfilling. I sincerely hope at least one of my learnings will have a positive impact on you and the lives of those you love. It is important for you to know that my desire for you to benefit from my learnings is not altruistic. I wish this for you because I believe my life is intertwined with yours; and everyone else's for that matter. Although intertwined, our lives are not at all co-dependent, nor should they be.

This book is not written as a typical story with a beginning, middle and end. I have instead attempted to mimic the process of self-healing that I experienced. I have written the book in this way to give you a tangible, real-life example of what your journey will be like if you choose to pursue it. Each chapter reveals something that was previously unknown to me. It was not until I found a critical mass of these learnings that I recognized that I held something of significance.

I have written this book in the form of a letter, from me to you. The letter has many sections; each attempting to convey one of the lessons I have learned during my journey. The learnings are sourced from my analysis of the memories and the events of my life. I think of each section or chapter as a glimpse into my life's journey and therefore, call them vignettes; a small impressionistic scene that focuses on one particular moment in my life. In this way, I am able to explain the significance of that memory on my journey.

In an attempt to make each vignette more readable, I have used italicized text to indicate an actual memory. Regular text is used for everything else, including my analysis. Whenever possible, I have written the memories as I remembered them; as unfiltered and raw as possible. In my voice, often in the first-person, present tense.

Please do not conclude that my life's journey is complete; it certainly is not. I have not yet embraced all of my memories, and I am not fully healed. This book is a means for me to assimilate what I have learned thus far. The very process of writing it is a powerful healing and learning opportunity for me. I hope it is for you as well. Every time I re-read and edit a section, I remember more and more details and am then able to heal another little piece of me. This book is also a 'way station' for me: a resting place where I can analyze, reassess and share my learnings with others. Sharing these learnings make them more valuable to me and hopefully to you. Maybe then, you too will start your journey.

I must caution you, however, that this journey will trigger thoughts of blame. Please try to free your mind from its shackles. Assigning blame will not fix a thing. I don't know if the following is a quote from me or someone else, but it sums up my view on blame... 'Blame others when you don't want change, blame yourself when you want despair.'

Before I go any further, let me introduce myself. I am a relatively typical guy in my mid-fifties. I'm industrious and compassionate. I live with my wife and twins in a suburb of an east coast city in North America. Most people enjoy my company. I mention this simply to say that I am not much different than you. Maybe older, maybe younger but very much the same.

To protect the privacy of those I love, I have written this book under a pseudonym and have changed the names of my family members and friends. I have also changed geographic locations and other potentially identifiable facts. I wish there were another way to preserve my family's privacy and simultaneously be true to you. But, unfortunately, there is no other option. I trust you understand their desire to remain anonymous.

Finally, I want you to know that I am not a medical professional and am therefore not qualified to give medical or psychological advice of any kind. It is my intent to recount my personal experiences and only offer information of a general nature to help you in your quest for personal growth. In the event you choose to adopt any suggestion implied or stated directly, neither the publisher, my psychiatrist nor I can assume any responsibility for your actions. Please, seek the services of a qualified medical professional before undertaking any suggestions herein.

memories

Without time we are no more; without relationship we have no purpose; without memories, we have no past. I have come to believe memories, relationships and time are the essentials of the human life experience. For most of my life, I only saw memories as learning tools that helped keep me from repeating the mistakes of the past. What I did not know is that memories are so much more. Memories give us a means for understanding the now, and they are the stuff that makes us who we are. I did not value my memories, and I don't want you to make that same mistake.

... I am in the family room of the house we lived in with my father. I am three years old. I had been watching the Mighty Mouse cartoon and got very excited. I was in awe of Mighty Mouse. I still smile whenever I remember his grin and his confident pose of courage.

I grabbed a blanket or towel and held it around my neck like a cape. Then I ran around the room as fast as I could. The cape would not flap as I ran. I wanted it to flap in the wind like Might Mouse's cape. I ran out the front door, around the yard and jumped into a tree well. My cape flew! I was happy.

It was cold that morning, and there was dew on the bricks of the well. I tried to climb out, but I could not. I could not see out of the well either. I was trapped and all alone. I started to cry. My brother and sister came and laughed at me. My mother came and spanked me. I never watched another episode of Mighty Mouse again. Not because she forbade it, but because I was a quick learner.

I believe this memory and the one I shared a few pages back, serve as the foundational events of my life. I do not know if there are other more fundamental memories. But for now, that does not matter. I can trace my world view, my thought processes, my decisions, fears and behaviors to those two relatively trivial events. It has taken me a lifetime to achieve this level of understanding.

For the vast majority of my life, those two memories were simply events of little consequence. They were neither good nor bad. They were there, in the recesses of my mind with no emotional attachments. They were the only memories I had before the start of 1st grade, at the age of five. I knew them only as my earliest memories.

I now see those two events as beautiful gifts. They are a part of me; a fundamental, core part of me. They taught me how to survive and prosper in the life I would eventually lead. I will later learn; they formed one of the many pathways to love. Love of self as well as the love of others. These words still sound corny to me. But I know, without any doubt, they are true.

There was something else about those two events that differentiated them from all my other memories. They would flash into my consciousness frequently and at unpredictable times. I did not understand why. There was nothing unusual or odd happening in my life when those memories would pop into my head. Just everyday things like making a decision or wrestling with a dilemma or maybe a confrontation with someone. It would even happen during mundane activities like driving or showering. There was no rhyme or reason for the memories to pop into my head, or so I thought. I can only tell you that those two memories popped into my consciousness more and more frequently as I got older.

learnings

What did I learn from those two foundational events? How can relatively minor events have such an impact on my self-identity and self-awareness? How did those learnings impact the way I have lived my life?

The Mighty Mouse event taught me a variety of things. I learned that I must be courageous and confront all threats. I must do so without the appearance of fear, and I must do it alone because no one else can or will. In hindsight, I now realize, that the Mighty Mouse memory flashed into my consciousness whenever I was not letting anyone know how scared I was, how alone I felt or when I accepted responsibility for something difficult because no one else would. That memory was somehow triggered whenever I was courageous or confronting threats. Later on, I will discuss memory triggers and describe how they can be used to overcome emotional blindness.

The memory of me huddled in the dark, taught me that my need to be comforted is not important to those I love or to those who love me. Emotions are the source of pain. I also equated need and vulnerability, with disappointment and rejection. I concluded that need and vulnerability were a weakness. I learned that I alone must find a way to comfort myself. I knew that I must never be vulnerable.

Those two events were not only impactful in their own right, but each reinforced the learnings of the other. I was happy and proud that my cape flew yet I was punished and ridiculed for having those feelings. The core of my identity was forged from those two events. I became a man of steel: Completely self-reliant, unaffected by my emotions, yet empathetic, just like Mighty Mouse.

I equated fantasy and play, with punishment and shame. From that point forward, I rarely, if ever, engaged in fantasy play. That was a significant day for me because I not only lost my childhood innocence, I also developed a way of avoiding emotional pain. The core of my self-identity took root, and a life-long pattern of behavior for ignoring pain was firmly established.

Another behavior of mine is to vacation at Disney World as often as possible. Writing this section has allowed me to associate it with the lack of fantasy play during my childhood. Many other questions are answered now that I have made this critical connection. I am certain, my next Disney World experience will be very different from all the rest.

Those two memories also introduced me to the notion of self-awareness beyond the now. Typically, we use the term self-aware to differentiate ourselves from other people and from our environment. I feel this way, at this point in time, and I do or do not, impact the rest of the world. Previously, I believed that there was no relevant time dimension to being self-aware. I experienced each moment as it is; separate and distinct from my distant past. I believed that I experienced each moment in the now connected only to the immediate past and future. My past was of interest to me only if it could inform me of previous successes or failures so that I could improvise strategies for success.

The thing I learned is that there is also a time dimension to self-awareness. I now know that my distant past is connected to the present through the filters of my mind, heart and soul. But what does this really mean? Do you have a fear of heights; demons; or small enclosed places? Think of that thing that frightens you to the core. Do you remember the event that caused you to develop that fear? What happens when you are suddenly confronted with something that triggers that fear? Do you feel it almost as if you are back to that time and place? Your fearful response to the current event is instantaneous. The now is directly connected to the past and you are completely unaware of this connection, but are acutely aware of the fear.

As I mentioned before, memories were popping into my mind more and more frequently; I just did not know why. Eventually I realized that the memories were popping into my head as reminders of very specific emotional responses. Emotional responses that occurred in the past as I was experiencing the current event. As such, these reminder memories act as surrogates or templates for emotional responses. In this way, I don't feel the emotion in the now. Instead, I only remember the past event. My mind uses these emotion templates to protect me from the pain of an emotional response. It does this by presenting me with the memory rather than flooding me with the feelings associated with the event. My mind is performing an extraordinary act of protection while also keeping me emotionally blind. Later, I will discuss in more detail the concept of emotional blindness and describe its power, benefits, and limitations.

Having said all that, I have been living my life unaware of any of this. I have been completely ignorant of the power of the human mind and its capacity to make these automatic associations. All I knew was that those two memories kept on popping into my head more and more frequently. I did not know why and I did not care. I did not know that my subconscious was trying to wake me up and I was oblivious to the fact that I was trying to feel and heal.

inadvertent effects

We all know that the events of our lives have a lasting impact. But significant events take root and affect us in ways that are not only unimaginable but unknowable. The goal is to uncover the unknown so that their impact may be understood.

... I am in a truck. A man is driving. I am sitting on my mother's lap crying. Eventually, I fall asleep and wake up in a different place.

I later learned that man was my uncle. He was driving my mother, brother, sister and I from our home in Pelham, New York to my grandfather's house in Newark. It was the house where my mother spent her youth as an Italian immigrant. It was located in the North Ward; a Newark New Jersey neighborhood. We lived there with my grandfather on the 3rd floor. My mother's sister and her family of four lived on the first floor. I was three years old, my sister was five, and my brother was seven. I was in a strange, frightening place.

... My twins were each given their first set of LEGOs™ by a relative one Christmas. They quickly constructed the scene on the box and then came to me requesting help. They could not finish the scene because some pieces were missing. I told the kids it would not be possible for them to complete it because there are not enough pieces in the box. They protested and wanted me to go to the store and buy them some more. I was angry at LEGO and a little sad. They obviously had a fantastic product demand model, but not a very satisfying toy. I never bought my kids LEGOs, and it angered me whenever my wife did. She bought

them lots of LEGOs. I thought they were a waste of money.

Weeks or even months after that Christmas, the picture of a little boy sitting alone playing with LEGOs popped into my head. It was a new memory for me, but it began to happen often. At first, I only recognized the room. Eventually, I accepted that the little boy was me. The memory was also accompanied with mild feelings of frustration, anger and sadness, but the feelings were not connected to anything.

... I am three or four years old sitting alone in the middle of the living room of the 3rd-floor apartment. I am playing with a very small LEGO set that had a handful of pieces, a window, and a door. I am trying to make a house with the LEGOs. I can make a tiny enclosed box with the pieces, but I cannot make a house. I desperately wanted to make a house. A house with a roof, a window, and a door. I try and try and try to make a house, but I cannot. I try to make a windowless house with just a door and a doorless house with the one window; nothing works.

"I want to make a house, mama," I remember the plea but not the answer. *I asked many times.*

As time passed, I realized that the memory was triggered whenever I saw LEGOs. It was also triggered whenever I was not being heard.

... It was a hot summer evening in the early sixties. A truck with an amusement park ride on its bed parked down the street. Fun music was blaring from it and excitement was everywhere. The neighborhood kids and their parents had surrounded the truck. We were there too.

A dozen or so children and their parents climbed aboard the back of the truck. There were two people in each seat and a bar in front of them to hold. The man collected a dime from each and shut the door. He pushed the button, and the seats began to move around a center console: Like chariots at the Circus Maximus. The seats glided down one side of the center console and then whipped around the corner and up the other side. The kids shrieked as they were flung around the ends.

"We can't afford it, Anthony, we don't have enough money."

I did not ask her again even though I knew that there were lots of dimes on the top of my mother's dresser.

Why do I see myself as an inconsequential pauper? Why is my biggest fear the loss of my job and the lack of income? The answers are now obvious. I just wish I was aware enough to ask those questions decades ago.

ignore not, force not

I know that you too have experienced events in your life that have scarred your very essence. Those events are often too real and painful to remember. But they are not lost. They have been etched somewhere within you, hidden and ignored. Until recently, I did not realize that I had hidden memories. I did not know that I had pushed them into my unconscious. I was completely unaware of the fact that I have avoided and ignored most of the scarring events of my life.

It amazes me that I did not know that I had these scarring memories because I took pride in the belief that I knew everything I needed to know about me. I honestly thought that I remembered every, single, possible thing about me and my life. Eventually, however, I realized that I had lost some of my memories. In fact, there are missing months if not years. I had even rewritten the story of my life so that the scarring memories fit a narrative that was more palatable to me. The extraordinary thing about the realization that I had rewritten my story is that I had no idea I had done so. The frightening thing is that the revised story may be so far removed from the real me that I may not recognize myself.

Re-writing the story was a matter of me cataloging the memory with incomplete or false facts. The lost memories were not actually lost; they simply did not exist. 'Lost' implies you know you had something, and now you do not. I never lost the memory because I never recognized the event as important enough to be remembered. In fact, I did not realize that the event was painful at the moment of its occurrence. My ability to become emotionally blind was both powerful and instantaneous. The result of this is a memory devoid of pain; a memory without emotion. I will later learn that I did indeed record all of my memories; they do indeed exist within me. The memories have been cataloged in my subconscious mind, preserved in totality along with their emotions. A very frightening, yet reassuring thought.

As time passed, memories began to surface. Like my two earliest memories, they just innocently popped into my head. Even the 'lost' memories entered my consciousness in a hidden form of some sort. Sometimes they appeared as a random thought with no context. Other times as a random feeling of fear, anxiety, sadness or anger during a situation where I should not be feeling that way. In all cases, however, the memories did not surface in their entirety. Nor did I even realize they were of any consequence.

The journey I mentioned in the beginning of this letter was the means by which I learned to embrace those painful memories. I no longer fear most of them, and I want you to know that it is possible for you to not fear yours. I want you to see, understand and cherish the painful events of your life. I want you to reach the point in your life's journey where you no longer need to shy away from them or compose a narrative about them. I want you to know your painful memories in intimate detail. But know them in their purest form. Know them without the biases, filters or covers we drape them in as protection from the fear and pain they have caused. Learn the who, what, where, when and why of them. Feel them. Take them into your heart and cherish them, as I cherish mine. It is possible, and it is very empowering.

I know that confronting the painful events of your life is not an easy thing to do. It is, in fact, an extraordinarily frightening and difficult thing to do. But I assure you, it is one of the most direct ways for you to love yourself. I have learned that embracing my memories in this way is an act of self-love that has allowed me to experience life in ways that were previously unimaginable. I now see beauty, feel joy and have hope where there was none. I now believe that loving yourself in an unconditional way, is a prerequisite to living a life of significance. I must caution you, however, to pursue these memories slowly and with care. Listen to yourself. If you are not prepared to uncover something; don't! It is OK to let it go. Don't push it. Do not force things you are not yet ready to do. The act of consciously recognizing that you are not ready to address a particular item is, in and of itself, an act of self-love. Why; because you are both protecting yourself and acknowledging the realities of the painful thing. On the other hand, growth only occurs when you stretch yourself beyond your norm. You must find the balance.

... "No force," said my grandfather as he handed me a puzzle. It was made of two pieces of metal tied together like a knot. I was a little boy at the time, under the age of five. I took the puzzle and played with it. I twirled it on the table top. I even tried to make it stand up. My grandfather picked up the puzzle and separated it into two pieces. He then put the pieces down on the table. I thought it was a magic trick and tried to put it back together but I could not. I gave the pieces to my grandfather who magically combined them.

My grandfather handed me the puzzle and said, "No force."

I don't know how many weeks or months it took for

me to figure the puzzle out, but I eventually did. The solution was to find the path that allowed the pieces to be entwined with ease. This lesson of 'no force' has been with me since that day. I learned that even the impossible is possible. That forcing something may actually make it more difficult. I also learned perseverance, but more importantly I learned that I can be a magician too.

first step

Sometimes you need to step out of your comfort zone and trust your inner voice. I know that is a cliché, but I can't think of another way to say it. As time has passed, I have created a life with fewer and fewer options. I have purposefully limited my choices to avoid the dangers and pitfalls uncovered throughout my life's journey. An easy and extreme example of this is that my life's path does not include the use of drugs. It also does not include horror movies or attending social events. Excluding drugs from my life is clearly 'wise'. But parties and neighborhood cookouts??? Obviously, some of the things I have avoided have not been in my best interest.

... *"Hi Linda, how are you?"*

Linda and I have a long history. I used to work for her at one of the largest computer manufacturers in the world. Eventually, we started a software business with four other people. I was the founding CEO, and Linda was responsible for sales. We sold the business after about two years and then worked for the company that purchased us. Eventually, we went our separate ways. Linda is a very smart, analytical and definitive person. I know, when she has come to a conclusion, it is well thought out. I respect her and trust her judgment.

Having said all that, Linda and I had some fairly brutal arguments. We were both left scarred and kept our distance. It turns out that Linda and I had a love/hate relationship. She represented my mother, and I represented her father. Even though a friend had previously introduced me to the dangers of re-playing unhealthy family relationships with others, I was unaware that I was doing it with Linda.

"What a pleasant surprise, thanks for coming," I said with a heartfelt smile.

We had an open house, and Linda came to reconnect. We had not seen each other for years. As we discussed our lives, it became evident to me that there was a calm in her that I had never seen before. I opened up and told her that I had come to realize that my life was muted, and I was emotionless. I also told her that I was seeing a shrink to find out why.

Linda had started her journey many years earlier.

"Tony, you have to come to this three and a half day workshop with me. I will be one of the facilitators."

"What is it about?" I asked.

"It is about what we have just been talking about; it is about healing."

I asked her where it was going to be held and how much it would cost. It was more than I wanted to spend, and it would require I stay overnight at a hotel for a few nights. I was very hesitant, but I saw a palpable change in her.

"Is it a massive shrink session?" I asked.

"No, not at all. It is run by a mystery school that focuses on bridging the chasm between the inner sacred and the outer life we live. You will be able to see your life from a different perspective. You will see the unhealthy patterns that have

*governed your world. It will also help you open your heart so
that you can live a fuller life. A life without fear."*

*"Huh???" I thought. I was not the kind of person who shared
my feelings with anyone nor did I discuss my inner and outer
sacred life; whatever that was! But there was something very
different about Linda, I could see it on her face. Even at the
worst of times with Linda, I always trusted and respected her
judgment.*

"OK Linda, I am in, how do I sign up?"

Agreeing to attend this workshop was significant for
me because it took a leap of faith. Something I never did.
I always weighed the pros and cons, risks and rewards.
But this time was different. I was at the point in my life
where I knew my default behaviors were not working for
me any longer.

*... That evening I went to the website and got a little scared.
The workshop was clearly not for me. It was for those touchy,
feely, new-age people who, only want love, and believe mankind
is in the process of ascending into the 4th dimension.*

*I called Linda and said in an accusatory way, "Linda, is this
a cult?"*

*"No, Tony. I understand your fear, it is not a cult at all;
quite the opposite. It has truly had a transformative effect on
me."*

*Had I asked Linda that question, in that way during the
height of our conflicts, she would have blown her stack. It would
have set Linda off. But she was calm and understanding. She
explained how the weekend would go, and she answered most of*

my questions. But, there were questions that she did not want to answer because they would 'diminish my experience at the workshop.'

I still had huge reservations. I categorically realized I was putting myself in the hands of another person. Committing to this workshop meant I was allowing myself to be vulnerable. It was a frightening thought. There is no other person in this world, other than my wife, who could have ever convinced me to go to a workshop about my feelings.

... A few months later I walked into the room where that workshop was being held. It was a Thursday evening in November, around 6:30 pm. It was a very large room, and I was surprised at how warm and cozy the room felt given its size. There were burning candles on an altar.

"A frigging altar," I thought. "I am a Catholic, and there is only one altar I know of, and it is not that! I am not going near it; ... just in case."

Two rows of chairs were arranged in front of the altar like an arch. There were two more rows of pillow chair things called BackJacks. They were arranged in front of the chairs also in the shape of an arch. Then I saw boxes of tissue paper on the floor. There was one box every 4th chair or so. Those boxes of tissues were the biggest surprise for me.

"Oh my, God," I thought. "How can I survive 3.5 days of people whining and crying about their shit?"

As people started to come into the room, I noticed that they were all different ages, races, religions, sexual preferences. Most of them looked like the touchy feely type. Some were odd, and a few looked lost.

"I've got to find a seat near someone who looks normal," I thought.

I began labeling people and figuring out who I was going to avoid. I did not want to be in any small group activities with them. I began to doubt if I could last the entire weekend. There were only 5 or 6 normal looking people out of the 100 or so that were there. I was screwed.

I decided if this workshop turned out badly, I would use the time as an opportunity to learn how these types of people think and what motivated them. If analyzing them did not work, I would think of it as a live Jerry Springer show. I promised myself to not get sucked into any group-wide discussion.

By the third night of the workshop, I had experienced joy: True, pure joy. I had giggled like a little boy in glee. I had not felt joy that deeply since the birth of my twins, 20 years ago. During that workshop, I had grieved the death of my father and the loss of the family that never was. I also kept my promise and did not say a thing to the larger group.

I left that evening exhausted, but happy that we would have one more day together. As I drove to my hotel room, I remembered the smiles, and the laughter and the tears, and the anger and the compassion and the strength and the wisdom of all those beautiful people. There were no weirdos in the room any longer.

I attended this workshop a year and a half ago. It was the first time I had ever done anything like that before. It was also the first time I knowingly saw and felt me.

harmful protection and truthful lie

We all have stories that rationalize our lives to ourselves and to others. We have created our stories in such a way that they fit our world view regardless of whether or not they are factually accurate. Our stories only need to be faithful to our definition of self, not to reality. Furthermore, our stories do not truly define who we are. Instead, our stories only define who we want to believe we are and who we want others to see.

Earlier, I declared that I can now trace my world view, thought processes, decisions, fears and behaviors to two, very early memories. That is both a bold statement and a damning indictment. Bold, in that I believe I know which events of my life were formative. That is an extraordinary feat. It is also a damning indictment in that those two events are not unique or horrible. My life must have been relatively easy and simplistic if two, seemingly ordinary, if not trivial, events were indeed foundational. Haven't most North American children mimicked their favorite cartoon character and been embarrassed or reprimanded for doing so? Is there a child that does not have early memories of their parents fighting?

Why then, do I believe those two events are fundamental to who I am and how I have lived my life? The easy way to answer that question is to devote significant time, and many pages, telling you my story. The story I have memorized and delight in telling. The story I have constructed about my life to explain the reasons why things are the way they are. The story that rationalizes every decision I have made and everything I have done.

The story that is oblivious to the fact that I was emotionally neglected as a child due to my mother's depression. The story that constructs a narrative about me which justifies my life and even, my existence. I have dozens and dozens of tales to tell in support of every aspect of my life. Some of them are funny, others are amazing, and most are sad. With my story, I can describe in detail how my childhood events have lead to the milestones, achievements, and failures of my life. I can explain each step, every decision, and my thoughts at the time. I can describe how things logically flowed and why each event was impactful. I can describe how and why I see the world the way I do and how I have therefore constructed my self-identity. My story allows me to emphasize the good parts; rationalize my failures, ignore those situations where I am at fault; and forget those realities I am unable to face. You know this story well; you have one too.

Ultimately, the story that describes why and how those two events are foundational does not matter. The thing that matters is that those two memories opened me to self-awareness. Through those memories I was able to make connections, see through the blindness and feel. They sent me on my journey.

The details of the story are not nearly as important as the connections the story has to your memories. Understanding those connections is key. Imagine yourself as a gem stone. Just like the surfaces of a gem, your story is multi-faceted. Each facet presents the different ways you see yourself and the ways you want others to see you. Each facet interacts with all the other facets of the gem, even those facets that are not touching each other. The next memory will give you a glimpse of me through one of those facets. It is a part of my story that positions me as a victim of circumstance who is willing and able to overcome the financial hardships that resulted from my father's death.

... "My old man is an asshole," declared a college classmate who had just spent the weekend in Bermuda.

"Why?" asked the girl he was sitting with in the cafe.

"He won't put any more money in my account. I have to wait until the end of the month."

"Oh God! Don't I wish I were you," I thought. I had to hurry and snarf down my lunch so I could get to work on time. It was a 21-mile drive.

I was working my way through school and paid for all of it including my living expenses. I worked 50 – 70 hours per week in the summers and 20 – 30 hours per week during the school year. I loved the work and hated school.

As I drove to work, I kept thinking about that kid. How lucky he was to spend the weekend in Bermuda while I had to work 11 hours that Sunday. That kid had no idea about the real world. If my father had not died, I would have had the money to go to Bermuda too, but I would not have done something so frivolous. It was a waste of time and money.

That kid was not unique. There were many privileged kids at the university I attended. There was even a princess in one of my classes. I still remember her fingernails. They were the longest I had ever seen. According to the girl sitting next to me, someone dressed her every morning because she could not button her blouse.

For 21 miles, I kept saying to myself, "I can't wait till we graduate, and he is across a negotiating table from me. I am going to take Bermuda Boy to the cleaners."

There were many times in my life when I would say to myself or others, 'If only my father hadn't died. I would have X and my struggle would not be so great.' Like paying for my college education, for instance. Or when I started a business and cash-flow was hard to generate. There were also times of distress where I would say the same thing. As a teenager, I was attacked by someone with a screwdriver and barely fought my way through it. Afterward, as I was gathering my composure, I wished my father had not died because I would not be living in an inner city neighborhood. Finally, I would often wonder about the opportunity cost resulting from having to do things that Bermuda boy never had to do.

For the majority of my life, I believed that my 'lot in life' was dictated by the lack of wealth. Had my father lived, his businesses would have been worth at least a billion dollars. Implicit in that belief is the idea that I could never reach my full potential because of the wealth that disappeared with his death.

My thoughts and analysis of my 'lot in life' are all logical and reasonable. They make sense, and they helped me deal with the struggles I encountered as I grew up. Part of my rationalization process included the acknowledgment of the things I learned that I would have never learned if my father had lived. I convinced myself that I benefited greatly from having to grow up with minimal resources; in the inner city with a neglectful mother and no father. This story of financial loss and the associated rationalizations contributed to my self-identity, and it formed one of the many facets of my self-image.

The story that I created is based on many factual truths. So much so that it defined me as well as other members of my family. But it was based only on a part of me. I hung on to that story until a few years ago when I came to the realization that my lot in life was ultimately determined by something much more fundamental and valuable than money. That realization was astounding. It was also liberating and very frightening because I no longer had the protection of my story. I felt naked and vulnerable without the story to justify and rationalize my life. I was frightened because I could no longer avoid the truth. I could no longer justify my decisions and behaviors as logical, reasonable responses to the fact that I grew up without a father, limited resources, and an absent mother. I could no longer hide behind the shield the story provided me. Nor could I continue to use it as the framework on which I established my self-identity. My story was both crutch and shield. It protected me and weakened me at the same time. One of the many profound things I learned during my journey.

find yourself by letting go

Telling you my complete story will be of little value to you because it is not factually accurate. It will only provide insight into the person I want you to see. It does not describe the real me and it will give you a biased view of me as well as the circumstances in which the story is told. As such, my story will allow me to continue to hide from the reality of who I am. I don't want to tell that story anymore because my journey is about finding the real me and learning to love that person.

However, for the purposes of this letter, I have no choice but to tell you bits and pieces of my story, so that I can describe both my journey and what I have learned about my self-identity. Therefore, I will recount little vignettes of the experiences that contributed to my definition of self. As I recount these events, I will also try to describe how those vignettes have shaped me and my journey. I will do that within the context of the learnings my journey facilitated. In this way, the fallacies of my story will become evident.

Please keep in mind that the vignettes I will present are not in the order that they occurred or in the order I remembered them. Unfortunately, they did not happen in any logical sequence. Instead, the vignettes happened randomly over many years. This letter organizes the vignettes into sets of related events as if they occurred in the proper chronological order. In this way, it will be easier to describe what I have learned and why it is important.

Another way to describe this is: For me to find the

treasure, I had to learn many things. I learned those things over many years through my life experiences. But my life experiences occurred in the order determined by fate, not in the linear sequence required to learn the things needed to find the treasure. Furthermore, the memory of those events popped into my head randomly. So one learning may be the culmination of events that occurred over many years, and the events did not happen in sequential order. Sometimes a single event would contribute to multiple learnings. This required me to remember the different events and link them together to form specific learnings. The term 'multi-factorial' seems to best describe the remembering and linking of many seemingly independent events.

There is one other critical thing I have learned about my story. That is; I had to let go of my story. Healing and learning required me to free myself from it. I could no longer use my story as a crutch that rationalized the decisions and events of my life. Nor could I use it to validate my self-identity. Ultimately, I had to allow my self-identity to evolve without the safety and protection my story provides. That does not mean I rejected my story or 'threw it away'; not at all. It simply means that I had to find out how my story defined me so that I could uncover the real me. Understanding the impact of my story on my identity is an important concept that needs emphasis. I had to find out how I used my story to define myself so that I could unveil my true identity. Only then, could I understand and more accurately describe me.

I have come to believe that uncovering the realities of my story is critical to the healing process. Having done some of this, I know it is necessary even though it is both difficult and frightening.

obvious, yet invisible

The most amazing thing about the human mind is that it possesses all that is needed to heal. However, few of us know that. We also don't know what is relevant, and we are unable to perceive the things from our past that are significant. Just as the famous sketch of the 'young girl / old woman' eventually reveals its truth; so too will your inner soul.

... "Do you think you are depressed?" asked my wife.

"No, I don't think I am... I saw a shrink when I was 23 or 24, remember? I've told you this story many times before. I wanted help transitioning into manhood. I knew something was missing in my life because I did not have a father."

My father died the night of the 1965 northeast blackout. It was about two years after my mother moved us to Newark. He was 33 years old. I was 5.

A few days or even a few week's later, my wife started the conversation again, the exact same discussion. This conversation repeated again and again until, like most men, I acquiesced and went to a shrink to appease her.

"Why are you here?" asked my psychiatrist.

"My wife thinks I am depressed, and I couldn't take the nagging anymore."

After we had discussed my medical history and my family relationships, etc. my psychiatrist asked me about my childhood.

"I have very few memories from before the first or second grade. The few memories I do have are primarily about school, not about my home life. I don't even remember any birthday parties. Do you want me to tell you about my life starting from the 3rd grade? I got expelled from school that year."

My psychiatrist was attentive, but she did not give me any facial cues or body language to read.

"How about a memory before the 3rd grade?"

"Well then," I said, "I'll have to start at the very beginning. My first memory was of my parents arguing. I was 2 or 3 years old. We were living in ..."

As I told that story, her faced changed, ever so slightly. I saw compassion and acknowledgment in her eyes. The first and only non-verbal cues I saw from her during the first two years of therapy. One therapy session near the end of year two, I asked her why she did not give me any non-verbal cues. She told me that she practiced a type of therapy that required that of the therapist. I immediately remembered my first session with her. I told her that I would not have agreed to therapy if she had not let me see the compassion and acknowledgment in her eyes. She said that she remembered that moment and had tried very hard to not respond. She could not help it.

That was all I needed at that time: A hint that my story impacted her. That was the moment when I realized the importance of that early childhood memory. I did not know why it was important, but I did take note. From that point forward, whenever the memory of me, in my diapers, huddled in the dark, popped into my consciousness, I tried to figure out why. I tried to remember what was going on at the very moment the memory popped into my head. For years, I did this. I looked for a connection of some sort. I tried to find the trigger. But I just could not determine what was going on and why.

... The appointment continued a little longer, and she said "Well, Mr. Martino, I am not yet sure if you are depressed. I need more time and a few more sessions before I can make that diagnosis. Would you like to meet again?"

"Yes, I would."

Before I left her office, I took note that she had a bookshelf with kid's toys on the bottom two shelves and psychology books on all the rest of the shelves. She also had a small, wooden kid's table in the far corner with two chairs. The floor had wall to wall carpeting, a small Persian rug, and two full-size chairs for adults.

What did I learn from that first appointment? It turns out that I told my psychiatrist all of the essential pieces of information needed to understand how I have defined myself and why. But, at that time, I had no idea. I was not capable, nor was I ready, to unravel the puzzle that is me. I did not even realize that it would be necessary for me to do so. You see, I was not depressed; not even a tiny bit sad. I had a successful career, and I am very well liked and respected. I live in an affluent suburb; my wife is beautiful, and my twins are great. By every measure, all is well. Maybe a little dull or colorless but comfortable and certainly OK.

overwhelming boxes

Who in the world am I? Ah, that's the great puzzle.

Lewis Carroll

Impactful events of the past are stored in our memories with the life experiences and perspectives of our youth. As adults, those very same events will not impact us as deeply as they once did because our point of view has evolved and our coping skills have been honed.

... One day, a year or two into my therapy sessions, I walked into the doctor's office and looked down at the small Persian rug. The same rug I took note of during the very first appointment I had with her.

"Why do you have that small Persian rug?" I had no idea I was going to ask that question. I sat down, looked at the rug and blurted the question out.

My psychiatrist answered, "I don't know, it's just my rug. What is it about the rug that interests you?"

"It is a beautiful, intricate rug," I said. "You know, my life is like that rug. It has extraordinary detail, but I can't actually see the detail. It is as if my mind has all the puzzle pieces that make that rug but I can't find them all. The frustrating thing is I am only able to get one piece at a time. Random puzzle pieces that aren't even in any order. I wish I could at least get the edges."

That was when I realized I was on a journey to collect

the puzzle pieces of my life. I had no idea why I had asked her about that rug or why I had associated the rug to a puzzle and the puzzle to my life. But I did know that I liked the rug/puzzle metaphor. It worked for me. It meant I was beautiful, intricate, sophisticated, and I gave people comfort. It also meant I was solvable. After all, I have completed many puzzles. It just takes patience and a good eye for patterns.

That interchange also helped me to realize the importance of 'tuning in' when a random memory pops into my consciousness. That memory was a puzzle piece, and I needed to catch it. Then, like a hunter, searching for more clues, I had to determine what type of animal made those tracks.

After a while, my puzzle metaphor became less prominent, and a new image began to form. It was a complimentary perspective, not a replacement, however. This image contained boxes. Unopened, unlabeled boxes. The boxes were in a warehouse; a vast, dark, cold warehouse. The warehouse was so large that I could not see its walls or ceiling. It was so dark I could not see beyond a handful of boxes strewn against the hidden, yet larger, pile of boxes. A pile of boxes that filled the warehouse; a pile that had no shape or dimensions. There was no top, no sides, nothing but vastness. No matter how hard I looked, I could not see beyond a few of the closest boxes. I have no idea how many boxes there are. I only know they fill the warehouse. An immense warehouse. I also know that fear and loneliness lurk in that warehouse, somewhere in and around those boxes. I will not step into that darkness.

The door to the warehouse is open. It is always open. I don't know where the light comes from, but it is always there, by the door. I can also see a few boxes, neatly arranged, just inside the entrance. Those boxes are labeled. I have seen the inside of those labeled boxes, and I am comfortable with them. One of those boxes is labeled 'Might Mouse', the other is labeled 'My First Memory'.

... *"I am afraid I won't be able to control my emotions if I open a box."*

"Why?" asked my psychiatrist.

"When I was about 25, I went with my wife, who was my fiancée at the time, to visit my father's grave. I needed to do that before I got married. I don't know why I needed to visit him, but I knew without any doubt, that I had to go. I also knew I could not go alone. That was very odd because there was nothing I could not do alone. I was glad Beth was with me."

"I had not been to my father's grave in NY since the day of his burial some 20 odd years earlier. He was laid to rest in a mausoleum. All I knew was the location of the cemetery. My Aunt gave me directions to it. He was in a building somewhere in that cemetery. I did not know exactly what building or where he was interred."

"I did not cry when he died. For all intents and purposes, I have not cried since that time. I'll never forget his wake. I'll tell you about it sometime but first let me finish this story."

"It took an hour or so to drive from my aunt's house to the cemetery. We stopped at a flower shop across the street from the cemetery, and I bought some flowers. My plan was simply to say hello, tell him that I was getting married, leave the flowers, and say goodbye.

"The first thing I needed to do was find that building. The mausoleum where he was buried. Then I would walk around it until I found him."

"The cemetery was the biggest I had ever seen. It had many buildings. I have absolutely no memory of ever being there. The only memory I have of that day was the limosine we sat in and the flower cars. There we about six hearses loaded with flowers. All the cars were black."

"I drove through the front gate of the cemetery and took all sorts of turns. Somehow I found myself in front of the mausoleum. I have no idea how I knew how to get there, but I did. The mausoleum was multi-storey. I didn't even know what floor he was on. I walked in, holding the flowers in one hand and my fiancé's hand in the other. I only know this because my wife later told me she had grabbed my hand. Somehow, I walked straight to him. I had not been there since I was five."

"The moment I saw his name carved in the white marble I collapsed against it and sobbed. I wailed. I cried. For two and a half hours I cried. Eventually, my voice gave way and my eyes stopped making tears. I was exhausted, spent, weak, shaking and confused. Beth was by my side the entire time."

"That is why I am afraid to open a box. I will be overwhelmed, and I won't be able to stop crying."

My psychiatrist looked at me and said, "But you did stop crying."

She paused and then said, "I don't think you will be overwhelmed when you open another box. The box was created when you were a child. When you did not have the skills,

39

understanding, strength or emotional maturity you now have as an adult."

Even though I understood what she said and trusted her judgment, I was simply too afraid to open a box. It would take me years before I finally did.

My psychiatrist's response helped me make a critical connection. My boxes contained my emotions as well as the events of my life. My memories were not forever gone. They were somewhere in my warehouse in unlabeled boxes. All of that pain was hidden away. That is why the warehouse is so dark and cold. It is also why I feel so alone and afraid when I am in the warehouse. Just like I felt that morning after I had jumped into the tree well fantasizing about being Mighty Mouse.

Later I would learn that the warehouse stored all of my emotions. Not just the painful ones. I know, based on other early memories, that I became adepts at putting both painful and overwhelming events into boxes. The details of those other events are not important. The important thing is that those events reinforced the behavior of putting events and their emotions into boxes.

I think it is important for me to mention that I labeled those first two memories only a few years ago as a part of my journey. Those boxes are now neatly placed in the lighted section of my warehouse. (Please note that opening, labeling and organizing the boxes is not an overt act on my part. I am speaking metaphorically.)

Currently, those two memories are no longer hidden nor are they confined to their boxes. They are no longer too painful for me to bear, and I do not fear them at all. I embrace them. I cherish them. I have accepted them and their wounds. They are free to float into and out of my consciousness because they have become a fundamental, intrinsic part of me. I now realize those memories have helped mold me as well as the little boy within. I can see him in my minds eye. He is beautiful and needs my love. I will not abandon him. I will never abandon him, and I will love him with all his failings, fears, and foibles. Those memories, as well as all of the memories I have liberated, are entwined together with the boxed memories I do not yet know. Together, they make the beautiful tapestry that is me.

recursive identity

At the risk of describing a recursive paradox and being pedantic, I'll summarize the previous pages and describe what I do during my journey to understand and define myself...

My self-identity is the result of how the events of my life have impacted me. The memories I have of those events, may or may not be accurate because they are biased by the way I want to remember them. My 'story' is a creation of my self-identity. It is the means by which I remember the events of my life and the way I want others to see me.

I can't figure out how I actually define myself because the way I remember the events are not necessarily accurate. They are not accurate because the way I define myself colors everything about the memories. My self-identity even colors the way I experienced the actual events in the first place.

The preceding paragraph is a classic 'Catch 22' situation where a problem is not solvable without a prerequisite, but the prerequisite is only obtainable by solving the original problem.

'Catch 22' situations are often resolved by redefining the problem or by including a piece of information not previously recognized as relevant. The missing piece of information in this paradox is found by honestly acknowledging the feelings or emotions of an event at the moment of impact or when the event is remembered. That is why I now focus first on the effect or impact of the event rather than the details of what happened. I try to identify how I felt at the time of the event, or how I am feeling as I remember the event. I had to first learn to recognize that an event or the memory of the event was triggering an emotion. Then I had to figure out what I was feeling and why. This is an important process point for me to remember and a key to finding puzzle pieces. In the beginning, it was difficult for me to do because I was so very disconnected from my emotions.

Please allow me to repeat this for you... 'I now focus first on the effect or impact of events rather than the details of what happened. I try to identify how I felt at the time of the event, or how I am feeling as I remember the event. I had to first learn to recognize that an event or the memory of the event was triggering an emotion. Then I had to figure out what I was feeling and why.'

Previously, I described two foundational memories that defined me. I also know that many other events in my life have reinforced my definition of self. What I don't know is whether those reinforcing events are indeed reinforcing and true or whether or not they are biased by the fact that I have already defined myself in that way.

Confirmation bias is the tendency to search for, interpret, or recall information in a way that confirms one's beliefs or hypotheses regardless of whether or not the information is factually accurate. An easy way to understand confirmation bias is to recall the last new or used car you had purchased or were about to purchase. One of the surprising things is that there are a lot more people driving around in that car than you remember prior to your decision to buy it. You see your new car everywhere you go. In actuality, the number of people driving the car has not increased, your perception has.

I mention confirmation bias because it can be used

to invalidate your definition of self. Specifically, if self-identity is confirmed by those events and memories that are reinforcing, and one does not know if the memories are indeed factual, or the result of confirmation bias, then one must conclude that their self-identity is false and not based on facts.

Ultimately, I believe that it does not matter whether or not one's self-identity is reinforced by an accurate recollection of the events or via confirmation bias. The reason I believe this is because one's self-identity is what they think it is. It would only matter if one knowingly concocted their self-identity from untruths and then consciously ignored or rationalized the fact that they are lying to themselves.

observing everything, yet seeing nothing

I once was lost but now am found,

Was blind, but now I see.

John Newton ~ Amazing Grace

I wish I could give you a set of instructions or a formula that describes how I identified those two foundational memories and how I have found other puzzle pieces. Unfortunately, I cannot. I simply do not know everything that I do. I also think that the process is unique to each person. My way of doing it will most likely be different from yours. There are two techniques; however, that I believe are common to all and are important to learn. The first technique is called mindfulness. Mindfulness is a way of actively focusing your mind on the present, in a non-judgmental way. With mindfulness, you become acutely aware of the now. Mindfulness is used to address the fact that some problems cannot be solved from within the problem. You must first step outside the problem to see the problem. The second technique is simply to let it happen. Don't try to push or force yourself to analyze things. Have faith in yourself. Have faith in the power and wisdom of your mind. It will happen when you are ready for it to happen. I know this with certainty.

Here is an example of mindfulness. It occurred about a year ago when recalling the first visit I had with my psychiatrist. I was driving home, listening to sports talk radio when the music from the song 'Amazing Grace' popped into my head.

... What I hear in my head regarding music is not what the vast majority of people hear in their heads. For me, it is a jumbled mess and incomplete. There is just enough 'correct' music that I know that it is a song I have heard before but I usually, cannot name it and I certainly cannot sing it. I can't sing any song.

The same is true of the lyrics. In this case, the words 'Was blind, but now I see' were prominent. As a matter of fact, I could hear the singing of the words 'Amazing Grace', and then 'Was blind, but now I see'. Then it left my head. A minute or so later, I heard the singing of, 'Was blind, but now I see. Amazing Grace, but now I see'. Then it would leave my consciousness again. As I drove home, bits and pieces of those lyrics would come and go, singing in my head. At this point, I did not know I had recalled the song Amazing Grace.

By this time, I was adept at being mindful. I recognized that I was having an emotional response to the lyrics singing in my head even though I was listening to sports talk radio as I drove home. I focused on the discussion I had just had with my psychiatrist. In particular, I tried to remember the point in the conversation when those words first popped into my head. I knew those words were crucial to uncovering a puzzle piece. I also knew it was important for me to figure out how I was feeling the very moment the words came into my consciousness.

... As soon as I got home, I 'Googled' the lyrics that were popping into and out of my head. That is how I found out it was the song 'Amazing Grace'. I read and re-read all of the lyrics of the song, not just the ones that were in my head at the time.

That is when it hit me. I was blind during my very first visit with the psychiatrist. I had told her all the important pieces of information, but I could not see their relevance or importance. It was all there. But it was impossible for me to understand it. I was blind.

I also realized that it was futile for my psychiatrist to show me the puzzle pieces. It would not matter. I would not be able to internalize those puzzle pieces in their truest form. Ultimately, showing me the puzzle pieces during that first appointment and then explaining their importance to me would have had no impact on me.

Being mindful was the technique that allowed me to recognize there was something there. It helped me realize that I was sad as I heard the song and also, therefore, sad as I told my psychiatrist the story of my life that very first session. That mindful moment helped me learn a little bit more about myself. It also helped me to formulate the concept of emotional blindness.

There were two critical learnings that day. The first was that everything I needed to know to solve the puzzle, which is me, is in my head. The second was that I won't understand the puzzle or its pieces until I am ready and able. Please keep in mind that these two learnings occurred many times throughout my life. Sometimes the memories would repeat other times the learnings would be offered via different memories. But I was oblivious until that day. I always liked the song 'Amazing Grace' but I did not even know its title. I marvel at the power of the human mind and lament the many years I spent not tuning into my life.

Here is another memory that reinforces the idea that it is not possible to see or understand something until you are ready. The following waking-dream was triggered as I remembered a memory from one of the sessions I had with my first psychiatrist.

... *"I was in my car, a 1981 Plymouth Reliant. It was midnight blue with a white landau roof. It was not a convertible. It was a hard top. But the image in my head is of my midnight blue Plymouth Reliant as a convertible. My mother, brother, and sister are in the back seat, and I am driving. The top is down, and everyone's hair is blowing back as we drive along. In this waking-dream, I am not only driving, but I am also observing from the outside. Everything is in silhouette."*

"I was sad, very sad as I looked at them. I wanted desperately for my family to learn what I had learned from my sessions with that psychiatrist. I wanted to put them in my car, drive around and show them everything I had learned. They had to learn what I learned; I was pointing it out and explaining it to them as we drove by each learning."

"Then it hit me. They would not learn a thing. Putting them in my car and driving them around was a waste of time. They would never understand. It was like learning math. You can't learn how to multiply until you learn how to add, and you can't learn how to add until you learn how to count. They did not even know how to count. I had to let go of this wish and let them learn these things for themselves."

Although I figured out that my family would not understand or appreciate what I learned 30 years ago, I was not able to apply the learning to other situations until relatively recently.

I just realized something extraordinary as I am editing this section. It reinforces the power of the human mind and its relentless pursuit to heal. When I was 16 my mother taught herself how to play the guitar. The first song she learned was 'Amazing Grace'. That was also the first time I heard the song. When I got my first cell phone, there was an option to display a message when the phone is turned on. I chose the words 'Serenity, Grace & Peace'. I am in awe as I sit here writing to you.

cognizant unconsciousness

I don't want to give you the impression that my thoughts, memories, and conclusions came flowing out of me in a constant stream. Nor were they in any logical sequence. They just happened. It was very much like finding a lost little treasure in the attic. You find something by chance, marvel at it, then put it into a special place for use sometime in the future. That is what I did. I just lived my life, and stuff would happen. Memories would pop into my head, or I would feel something in the center of my chest for a fleeting moment. I'd make an effort to be mindful so I could save that little gem.

The process I used was very basic. If something popped into my consciousness, I would acknowledge it and try to remember what was going on at that exact instant. I'd tag it as an important thing to remember for my next therapy session and then continue what I was doing. I never consciously pursued it beyond that. Also, I was not in a continuous state of analysis. Far from it. I rarely dwelt on my memories during my normal daily life. Instead, I would have faith that the memories would be there, in my head when I needed them.

At my next therapy session, I would try to remember what I had tagged. If I were lucky, I would remember everything. Sometimes I would only remember a part of it. In either case, I would try to reconstruct the memory, my feelings and any other hints that may be laying around in the recesses of my mind.

There were also times when I would not remember anything other than something important happened a few days ago. I never got upset with myself for not remembering because I knew that I must not be ready. I also knew, however, that I would not lose the memory. It would always be there, in my warehouse, and I would eventually find it. Not by searching that big scary pile. Instead, when I was ready, it would just pop into the forefront of my mind, magically placed in the light of the warehouse, in an unopened box.

I rarely prepared for my therapy appointments. Sometimes, as I sat in the waiting room, I would try to remember what I had tagged. Most of the time; however, I would wait until the session started before I attempted to recall my memories. I did this consciously because I wanted my session to be free flowing and unfiltered. Thinking about the tagged events in the waiting room would dull their impact during the session.

When I drove home from a session, I would re-engage my life, and the therapy topics would become background tasks in my mind. In the world of computers, the work a computer does is called a task. There are two types of tasks. Foreground and background tasks. Foreground tasks are the main things a computer does. Think of them as the things you interact with and the things you see the computer doing. Background tasks do the other stuff. They don't require your attention, and the user does not even know they are working, but they are critical to the functioning of the computer. Background tasks are the work of the unconscious mind. Being mindful is a foreground task. After I tagged a memory and its feelings, I would move it from the foreground to the background. Then my unconscious mind would do the analysis. The results of that analysis would be unknown to me until I walked into the psychiatrist's office, and it all became a foreground activity again.

Finally, I don't dream very much. Only a few times a year. Although dreams have not yet been a source of learnings for me, I suspect they are a treasure trove. If you dream, keep a journal by your bedside and write the dream down as soon as you can.

feel not

One day I realized that I did not feel emotions in the same way everyone else did; I was flabbergasted.

... *"They are happiness, sadness, fear, anger, surprise, and disgust. Why can't you remember them?" asked a friend.*

"I honestly don't know. It frustrates me. Can you believe that I did not even know that music and art are man's way of manifesting emotions? I only figured that out a couple of years ago. Maybe that is why I can't remember a single song. I only ever remember a few words. Like the song, 'Feelings'. All I can remember is the title and the basic tune."

Feelings entered my consciousness in unpredictable ways as I got older, and they occurred much more frequently. Here is another mindfulness moment where an emotion became evident to me. This was the first time I realized that I felt an emotion, and it had something to do with a repressed memory. My guess is that it happened about five years ago.

... *"Last night, while watching a TV commercial, I felt something. It was odd, and I don't know what it was or why it happened."*

"What was the TV commercial about?" asked my psychiatrist.

"A movie, 'The Greatest Game Ever Played.' It is about a poor Irish boy who became one of the greatest golfers ever. Everyone was against him because he was not part of the aristocracy. What killed me was a vignette showing a man who appeared to

be his mentor. That man believed in him."

"What do you mean, it killed you?"

"I really felt something. It was very strong, but it only lasted for a millisecond."

"Where did you feel it?" she asked.

"Right here," I replied as I pointed to the center of my chest.

It was through discussions like these that I came to realize I did not allow myself to feel my emotions. The odd thing is that it was not a new revelation. For instance, I did not cry when I learned of my father's passing, nor did I cry at his wake or funeral. I did not cry when my tibia and fibula broke completely in half. I even set my own leg while on the soccer field. I have many memories of when I was in pain, frightened or sad, and I did not show anyone how I actually felt. You see, it was not that I did not feel, I did feel. I felt deeply, but I hid the feelings and stuffed them away. I did not let anyone see them, except for my wife.

oblivious avoidance

Living a dull, muted life with little color, taste or smell is what my wife saw in me. It was my coping mechanism, and I was completely unaware.

... *"Did you guys travel somewhere over New Years," asked a co-worker friend.*

"No, my daughter got sick, and I needed an extra day off."

"What happened, is she OK?" he asked.

"She became paralyzed on the 1st. It lasted about a day."

"What?"

"She was unable to move her head but could move the rest of her body. She said that her body felt heavy and difficult to move."

My friend looked at me in disbelief and said, "What? I don't understand what you are saying."

"Genevieve simply froze up and could not move. It doesn't really matter," I said. "She is OK now."

My co-worker stood there dumbfounded and then said to me, "Tony, you did not just buy toothpaste."

I was confused and asked, "Why are you talking about toothpaste?"

"Tony, I can't imagine that happening to Michelle. You describe it like you'd describe going to the store to buy toothpaste."

My reply was "That kind of stuff happens to us all the time. It's not a big deal. I need to go and finish my memo."

A week or two passed, and my friend asked me how my daughter was.

"She is fine, why?" I asked.

"I can't believe you Tony; she is not toothpaste."

"What are you talking about? She's doing fine. Everything should be OK."

My family had been through many crises over the years. We dealt with this one, like all the others. My twins have a systemic neuromuscular disease. It is rare, and there is no cure. My wife knew something was wrong with them from the very beginning. But our pediatrician thought she was an overly protective mom. During the early years, my wife collected all the pieces of information about their illness she could. She learned the science and pushed the doctors. She would not let them ignore the many small facts that were outside the norm and not explainable. My twins visited the emergency room too many times over the years. They endured 100s if not a thousand tests. Blood tests, genetic tests, MRIs, neurological tests, muscle tests, you name it; they have had it. Eventually, we were referred to one of a handful of doctor's in the world who could diagnose the family of diseases my children have. The emotional and financial toll were astronomical.

After a week or so, I was driving to work, and the toothpaste comment popped into my head. I realized my friend was trying to tell me that the absence of an emotional response to those events was odd. I knew he was right, and I tagged the memory for my therapy session later that week.

I don't remember if I had discussed the toothpaste memory during my next session or not. But I do know that I had figured it out. Specifically, I hid my feelings too well. I can stifle my emotions in such a way that people can't see them, and I don't feel them to their fullest extent. I was living a dull, muted life with little color, taste or smell. Not only was I avoiding pain, but I was also avoiding joy.

stifled emotions

This next memory is the first time I knowingly did not let anyone see how I felt. The problem is I did not realize the impact it would have on my life. Nor could I realize: I was a child trying to cope with my reality.

... *"Oh my, Anthony, why are you here?" asked Mrs. Kenny, my 2nd-grade teacher. I was glad to see Mrs. Kenny because I was one of her favorites. It was the beginning of the new school year. I was seven years old and in the 3rd grade.*

"I don't know." I looked down as she walked passed the principle's office. It was clear that she was disappointed in me.

I was sitting on the bench in front of the principle's office. My teacher had marched me down there first thing that morning. She sat me down, told me to sit there until my mother came to get me. She walked into the principle's office, then after a few minutes walked out and right past me. I was in trouble and was scared. I did not know why I was in trouble, what I did wrong, or what was going on. After a couple of hours, the lunch bell rang. A child brought me my lunch box, a carton of milk and my coat. I don't remember if it was a girl or a boy. I could not eat. I was too upset and scared to take a bite. I did not know what to do with those things other than leave them on the bench next to me. A few hours later, the bell rang. It was the end of the day, and the children filed past me. No one talked to me that entire day other than Mrs. Kenny.

Eventually, my mother came. She looked hurried. She went into the office and after a few minutes came out. She helped me get my coat on and took me home. When we got home, she asked me if I had threatened a boy with a dart. I told her I had not, but I had found a dart on the sidewalk as I walked to school that morning. I showed it to the boy sitting next to me.

My mother was a teacher, and she could not come to pick me up until the end of the school day. Many years later she told me her principle would not let her leave to come get me. I wondered why my aunt did not come to get me instead. She lived on the 1st floor of the same house where we lived. I never asked why. It was a horrible, frightening day. I had been expelled but did not know what that meant.

The next morning, my mother went to work and left me with my aunt and uncle. I heard my uncle on the phone. "What do you mean he did not cry?" I went back to school after a day or two.

I later learned that my uncle had called the principle and got me reinstated. It turns out that they believed I was guilty because I showed no fear, and I did not cry. To this day, I have no memories of that entire school year. Literally, not a single memory beyond that day sitting on the bench in front of the principle's office.

This memory is still very raw for me and was difficult to write. Obviously, it is a memory I need to process. I'll try to do some processing right now as I write so that I can share it with you.

I can remember the utter fear and dread I felt sitting on that bench. I remember it being an eternity. I never went to the bathroom that day, even though I needed too. I can feel fear, shame and dread as I write about the memory and I still feel it now. This morning, after re-reading that section, I feel almost the same as I did last night, but not quite as intensely. I have always known that I was afraid that day. But, I had never before associated shame and dread with that event. That is a new feeling for me.

What I need to do is become mindful. I need to clear my mind and let the fear, shame and dread become a part of me. I am not sure I can. I know I am not yet ready, but I will try. I will close my eyes and clear my mind of everything except for that memory and the feelings...

I was not successful. I tried to open and allow the pain into my essence but I could not. All of my defenses are up, and I am intellectualizing rather than feeling. Intellectualizing is my default behavior. It helps me avoid pain. I do this through the process of logical thought. I look at and analyze all of the events through reasoning. I do it devoid of emotion and as objectively as I can. Sometimes, however, intellectualization opens a doorway into my feelings. Let me give that a try...

Here are my thoughts: As I mentioned previously, I remember more and more detail every time I re-read or edit this letter to you. In this case, I had no idea that I had disappointed Ms. Kenny. I did not realize this until a few minutes ago when I re-read the previous passage. I knew how much I liked Ms. Kenny and how happy I was when she talked to me. But, I did not know that I saw how disappointed she was in me. I also did not know that it triggered feelings of shame.

When I think about this event, I can't believe how young I was. It angers me as I write this. I started 1st grade at the age of five so my mother could get a job teaching. We apparently needed money now that we were no longer living with my father.

I am angry, and I do not know who or what is causing my anger.

... This is my contribution to the family.

Wow! Those words just popped into my consciousness. A flood of emotion is seeping into my essence as I type these words. It is gone! The emotion was too intense for me to deal with, so I stopped it. I boxed it.

Boxing a memory is the phrase I use to describe what happens when I put a memory and the corresponding feeling into an unlabeled box. Once in the box, it is thrown into the warehouse where it is no longer a part of my consciousness. I don't want to give you the impression that the boxing process is overt. It is not. It happens instantaneously, and I do not do it consciously. In this case, I know that I started to feel an overwhelming amount of emotion about the words 'contribution to family'. Then I felt nothing. No emotion, it had disappeared. That is how I know that I boxed it and threw it into the warehouse.

For much of my life, I did not even know I was boxing my feelings because the boxing would occur faster than I could register the pain. At some point in my therapy, I figured out that I was boxing my feelings, and I was doing it before I could feel them. I do not remember when I had realized I was boxing things. I suspect I figured it out during the process of creating the warehouse metaphor.

family tenet

We are all born into a family dynamic and social context that shapes us. It is crucial to understand it, and its implications on our lives. In many ways, my extended family is quite successful. We have a very low divorce rate, we are lawyers, doctors, entrepeneurs, astronauts, scientists, inventors, mothers and fathers. So what is the big deal?

I have always known about this concept of contribution to family, but I did not associate it with that horrible day. This connection is new, and I don't yet understand it. I need to process it before I can heal. I am confident that I will figure it out when I am ready.

What does 'contribution to my family' mean? I have always understood that the family was more important than the individual. This concept is the core tenet or unstated norm of my extended birth family. The mandate of this tenet is that your personal needs are secondary to the needs of the family. 'Suffer in silence' is another concept associated with this belief. We have all uttered it to ourselves and each other.

I believe my mother's father was the source of this tenet. He became an orphan at the age of nine due to a series of tragic events that resulted in the deaths of his parents and some of his siblings. He and a few of his younger brothers and sisters survived in the farmlands of northern Italy by working for food and shelter. They prevailed by sticking together. Later, during World War I, he was one of the few soldiers who survived the German prisoner of war camps.

This tenet was further ingrained years later when my mother's birth family lived through the great depression. As Italian immigrants, life had been particularly difficult for them. They had little money in addition to the typical assimilation difficulties of being in a new country, learning the language and trying to understand the culture.

When my mother, her brothers, and her sisters became adults, they passed this tenet on to their families. It amazes me when I see it manifest in my cousins, aunts, and uncles during a holiday like Thanksgiving. The vast majority of it is very subtle; however, some of it is quite overt.

My wife was very aware of this unhealthy family norm. She felt it the moment she attended the very first holiday with my extended family. But she knew I was blind and could not see, so she did not overwhelm me with her reaction to it. Instead, she was always supportive of me. Every once in a while, she would ask me a question or two about why things were the way they were. She was giving me little hints but never pushed me to confront it. She only ever gave me love and support. I am very lucky.

There is a much larger and more complex set of beliefs and behaviors that supported this family norm. But, there is no need to share all of it in detail. The one thing that is important to know is that there was a clear line of dominance in my extended family. Each family member has their position relative to everyone else. My mother was the black sheep of her birth family so her children; me, my brother, and sister, were of less importance than my cousins. That meant their needs were met before ours. As the youngest, I was last.

I must address the concept of blame before we go any further. We often blame our family for our current situation. It is important to know that it ultimately does not matter who is at fault. As I quoted earlier, 'Blame others when you don't want change, blame yourself when you want despair.' Blame is just another means for hiding from yourself, casting you as the victim. It is the catalyst that feeds the narrative you have created to answer the 'why' question. Instead, try to accept and embrace your reality.

painful joy

A single event can impact you in multiple ways including feeling both the high and low of the same emotion.

... *"Uncle Vinnie, he is the most handsome baby I have ever seen,"*

I said that with a feeling of pride and joy like I had never before experienced. "You know how most babies are kinda ugly. Not this baby boy."

"That is great Anthony, what are you going to name him?" asked my uncle.

"Arell Salvatore, the bringer of light and savior."

"That is a great name, Anthony. It is good that you are honoring your father with his middle name."

Then I told him about my daughter and my wife. At that time, no one knew how dire Beth's health actually was.

I then called my mother, "Hi Mama the twins were born, and they are OK."

"Are they on ventilators?" asked my mother.

"Not yet, but I need to talk to the doctor because they want to put them on the ventilators. I am in the lobby of the NICU."

"What did you name them?" she asked.

"Arell Salvatore and Genevi ..."

"Oh no Anthony, you have to change his name. I don't like either one of them."

"No, mom."

"It is not too late Anthony. At least give him a better middle name."

I don't remember the rest of the conversation. I do know, however, that the joy I felt as I spoke to my uncle was the last time I felt joy deeply. Or maybe I should say, it was the last time that I felt intense, pure, innocent joy. For 20 years after that, any joyful event was muted.

my mother's son

Unhealthy patterns of behavior may be multi-generational and are often repeated out of ignorance. The key is to identify these unhealthy patterns so that the cycle can be broken.

... I sat down, smiled at my psychiatrist and then looked out the window. I often looked out the window at the sky and trees whenever I was processing something significant. I felt a deep pain and was also in awe at the insight that had just popped into my head.

"My father's death was not the thing that I lost," I said. "I mean, I did lose my father, and that was a big loss, and it definitely impacted my life. But the loss of all that wealth and opportunity is not the truly valuable thing I lost. The truly valuable thing was that I never allowed myself to have emotions. I am certain that all of the achievements of my life would have been easier to obtain and been more fulfilling had my emotional development been normal. It was not the money or the lost opportunity at all. It was the immature development of my emotions. I can't believe this."

I continued restating this, refining my understanding and giving examples. My psychiatrist listened. Near the end of the session, she said words to the effect... that conclusion sounds reasonable, but do not forget that your ability to stifle your emotions was critical to your survival. It served you very well. You needed it. It was, and is, a powerful and extremely valuable coping mechanism. Without it, you would not have survived and prospered as you have. It is quite remarkable.

That session was both inspiring and very sad for me. It was also the first real proof that I needed to free myself from the protection of my story. From that point forward, I slowly let go of bits and pieces of my story. I still cling to some parts, but I know that I will eventually liberate myself from what remains.

Ultimately, growing up without my father, and only having my mother's influence, resulted in me stifling my emotions and feeling inconsequential. Even though it is painful for me to admit, I must acknowledge, that I was emotionally neglected as a child. My mother was never physically abusive or anything like that. She was simply not available. My mother did not comfort and nurture me to the degree I needed. I honestly believe that I would have received more emotional support and nurturing had my father been in my life.

My mother was not a horrid person. She simply knew no other way, was depressed and repeated what she was taught. She had also grown up in a home without emotional support and nurturing.

I do not know much about my mother's mother, but I am under the impression that she was not a compassionate, nurturing woman. I have heard a few stories over the years from siblings and cousins about my grandmother's cruelty to my aunts and uncles, but my mother never spoke of her. My Grandmother had died when my mother was nineteen.

My mother knew how to survive, and she taught me that. She learned it from her father; the preeminent man of steel. But my mother was not capable of giving me more than what she had.

I am also certain my mother knew that she was 'blind

and could not see.' I know this because of the books she read and because she sought the help of psychiatrists for as long as I can remember. Unfortunately, she did not overcome her pain and died a few years ago.

ignored needs

Consider the possibility that you are not who you think you are.

... I was sitting in the kitchen of my wife's friend's house, and I said to her, "I hate people you know."

"What do you mean?" asked my wife's friend.

"Just what I said, I hate people."

"So you hate me too?" she asked.

"No, not you. Just everyone else."

"How can you say that? You are so nice and sweet and warm to everyone. Everyone loves you. Everyone wants to be with you."

I looked into her eyes and said, "That is exactly why. People exhaust me. They suck the energy right out of me."

Many months later I found myself in a theater with my wife, my twins, my wife's friend, and her son. We are there to watch 'A Christmas Carol'. I am bored and about to fall asleep when I hear Scrooge singing, "I hate people ..."

I perked up and smiled. My wife's friend bursts into laughter nudged my arm and said, "There you go, you finally found a friend."

What did I have in common with Scrooge? At the time,

I had no idea. As a matter of fact, I was not even aware enough to make any connections or even ask the question.

Did I, in reality, hate people? Of course not. My kindness and warmth are genuine. But I did avoid people as much as I could. I now believe that I 'hated' people because I allowed myself to be subservient to them. Not as a subordinate, but as someone who is less important. I placed my needs as secondary to the needs of family, friends, co-workers, and even strangers. I gave them time, warmth, and help without any recognition that there may be an effect on me. My family norm was the only way I knew how to be. I was that way with everyone, regardless of the impact on me.

I believe the family norm, combined with my two foundational memories, are the source of my feeling inconsequential. They are certainly not the only reasons, but the seed was sown into the fertile soil of that tenet. My self-identity developed accordingly.

People who know me will be shocked that I have always felt inconsequential. They see me as competent, capable, and usually the center of everything. People seek me out for help and guidance. It is my nature to be a leader and a teacher. In their eyes, I am anything but inconsequential.

finding connections

The stories we tell about ourselves are much more revealing than we realize. Identify the stories and the circumstances in which they are told.

... "I think I also need to tell you about my egg."

"Yes, please do." she said.

This discussion was during my first session with my current psychiatrist. Thinking back, I now realize how odd that statement was. She did not know anything about me and could have concluded I was a complete nut case.

... "Well, my egg is actually a part of my stone theory. I got it from my grandfather; my mother's father. He was a short, slight man of few words; but as tough as can be. He had to be tough to have survived his childhood. He was orphaned when he was about nine years old."

"He was not a mean, angry or harsh man at all. He was a strong, quiet man that expected virtue, independence and strength from you above all else. I knew; deep inside him was a loving, compassionate human being. Unfortunately, I rarely saw that side of him."

"If I had to describe my grandfather in one sentence, I'd say he was a man of stone. But I somehow knew he had a fragile egg in the center of his chest too. The egg in the center of his chest was just like mine, covered in an impenetrable, indestructible shell of stone. Thus my stone theory."

"What do you mean by a fragile egg in the center of your chest," she asked.

"Well, it's the only place where I can be really hurt. I have to protect it from everything at all times. That is why my shell is made of stone. You know eggs are pretty amazing things. Everything there is about a chicken is in the egg. Once you break that shell, the egg can't be put back together again. Just ask Humpty Dumpty."

As I write those words to you, recalling that memory, I have only now realized that my grandfather was the original man of steel. It is now clear to me that I modeled a significant piece of my self-identity after my grandfather. A man who I respected and loved. I am absolutely amazed at the fact that I did not know this until now. How could I have told my psychiatrist about my stone theory so many years ago, and not make the connection until today?

The recalling of this memory is a 'real time' example of how blind someone can be. I did not realize the impact my grandfather had on me. I honestly did not know that I modeled that piece of my self-identity after him. I have told my stone theory story hundreds of times, to many different people, in many different situations. But it was not until this time that I made the connection between my self-identity and my grandfather. Previously, I saw my grandfather simply as one of the many people who had some influence on my life. In particular, he was the source of my extended birth family's ability to be tough and invulnerable. He was also the source of the tenet that the family is more important than the individual. This tenet was never stated, but it was understood by all of us.

I remember spending alone time with my grandfather

during those first two years in the North Ward. He would bring me with him when he went to 'the club'. The basement of a friend's house where a bunch of retired Italian guys hung out for the day. He did not speak much or play with me, but I enjoyed being there with him. Until now, I had not recognized the degree to which he helped shape me. It is also interesting to me that I only have a handful of memories of him. But all of those memories are both positive and impactful.

... "Why won't you let me win?" I asked.

"Because it's not real."

This memory just popped into my head. I know with certainty that the conversation consisted only of those two sentences. My grandfather was very frugal with his words. I lost every single game of checkers I ever played with my grandfather. He never let me win, but he did show me the mistakes I made in a very matter of fact way: with few words and no blame or shame. This is when I could see the inside of his egg.

... "Why did you do that?" I yelled at one of my siblings as I swung my fist in retaliation.

I don't remember if this event was with my brother or sister.

"It's the grandpa pinch," replied my sibling with glee. "Do you still have a headache?"

The grandpa pinch consisted of pinching and then twisting a part of your body that had extra skin like the inside of your triceps.

"Yes my head is worse now, and my arm hurts too," I yelled.

My sibling then justified the pinch by saying, "If I tell grandpa that something hurts me, he gives me a grandpa pinch to make that pain go away."

"I know," I said. "But you did not have to do it to me."

My sibling smiled with evil intent and said, "If your head still hurts I must not have done the grandpa pinch correctly, so I need to pinch you again."

I'm not sure why that memory popped into my consciousness. I guess it was part of the 'suffer in silence' message and the 'be thankful for what you have because things can always get worse' philosophy that was prevalent in my household. In all honesty, I don't know what this memory is all about so I will tag it for another day.

Here is a suggestion on how to find a puzzle piece. Think about the parts of your story you tell most often. How do you feel immediately before you tell it? How do you feel as you tell the story? Why are you telling the story? What parts are you emphasizing and what parts are you avoiding? Remember, that answering these questions is not easy. I suspect you will have to tell that story many more times before you will be able to answer those questions and find your puzzle piece. Be patient with yourself, keep at it and don't forget to be mindful.

emotional intellect

There can be no knowledge without emotion. We may be aware of a truth, yet until we have felt its force, it is not ours. To the cognition of the brain must be added the experience of the soul.

Arnold Bennett

... Commander Spock and Dr. McCoy from the original Star Trek series popped into my consciousness during a pause in a recent session with my psychiatrist.

"Are people fundamentally emotional beings or are they intellectual, logical beings?" I asked.

"I don't understand your question."

"Well," I said, "you know how I intellectualize. Imagine a spectrum with intellectualization at one end and pure emotion on the other. I am on the intellectualization side of that spectrum. Right?"

"Oh, yes, you are," she said. "A person can't survive without emotions and feelings, but they do not need intellect."

Then I remembered a newsreel from the 1950s. I saw it many years ago at Disney World. It showed a dozen or so babies in cribs. A milk bottle was connected to wires and moved as if through automation to one of the babies. The baby reached for the bottle and grabbed it with his feet and hands. The announcer described how only one nurse cared for all these babies. He then praised the high-tech sophistication of the communist country that built this system.

The next thought was of college and my Sociology 101 class. I had learned exactly what my psychiatrist had just told me i.e. that we are emotional beings and will not survive without physical touch or emotional nurturing. I sat there, in the psychiatrist's office amazed that I already knew that people are primarily emotional beings.

Associating the newsreel and the sociology class together was simply a reinforcement of something I had already known. If I already knew that people are emotional beings, why then did I ask my psychiatrist the question, "Are people fundamentally emotional beings or are they intellectual, logical beings?" The answer is quite obvious to me now. Obvious, because now 'I can see'. I was, in fact, asking her if I am like everyone else, fundamentally an emotional being. But I knew the answer to that question too. I knew that I am indeed like everyone else, and I have emotional needs. But I knew this on an intellectual basis. I did not know it from an emotional basis.

Merging the intellectual knowledge with the corresponding emotional knowledge is the only way to ensure complete understanding. It is also the only way to heal. That is what I was trying to do in this case. I was trying to merge the two. It is now clear to me that merging the two will change how I define myself in a fundamental way.

I had asked that question as part of my process of redefining my self-identity. At the time, I did not realize I was redefining my identity. It is only now that I am more mindful that I recognize this fact. It is also important to know that every time you change your self-identity, you must be willing to alter or release one or more of the characteristics that currently define you. As I mentioned earlier, intellectualization is my default behavior. I know that I do it well, and it is part of my persona, i.e., the man of steel who can keep emotion at bay. The unfortunate thing is that this description of self is now in conflict with the fact that I am essentially an emotional being.

How can the man of steel be an emotional being? How do I reconcile this inconsistency? I have a few options:

- Continue to reject the notion that I am an emotional being and preserve my man of steel persona.
- Reject the intellectual part of me and replace it with the emotional me or
- Merge the intellectual and the emotional in some way.

I have learned that merging is often the right choice.

fearless heart

Wealth without Work

Pleasure without Conscience

Knowledge without Character

Commerce without Morality

Science without Humanity

Religion without Sacrifice

Politics without Principle

Mahatma Gandhi ~ Seven Social Sins

The concept guiding Gandhi's Seven Social Sins is the notion that one cannot know or appreciate something completely without also knowing its antithesis. Please re-read the seven sins again with an eye toward understanding how and why the words describing each sin are opposites. Also, note that the order of the words is not important. The message of 'Work without Wealth' is the same as 'Wealth without Work' because a person of wealth is unable to understand the value of his wealth if he did not work for it. The same is true if one does not understand the value of what they have earned through work.

This concept of knowing something through its antithesis is fundamental to our ability to find our inner-self, and it is not limited to the seven aspects of life noted by Gandhi. It is also true for all aspects of our human experience.

... *"The heart workshop was profound," I said to my psychiatrist as I walked into her office.*

I had just returned from two weeks in Arizona where I attended a workshop that was about initiating the heart chakra. A chakra, according to ancient Indian teachings, is an energy center within the human body. The heart chakra is one of the 7 primary chakras and it is where we send and receive unconditional love. Before this workshop, I thought that chakras were total and complete BS. I even questioned the wisdom of going to a two-week 'heart conference.' I feared that it might be a ruse to initiate me into a cult. So much so that I had written a note to my wife and psychiatrist that gave them the authority to commit me if they believed I had become a member of a cult while in Arizona.

Why did I go to this two-week workshop if I believed it had the potential of being a cult? The answer is simple; the workshop had the potential of moving me further down my journey, closer to my goal. It was a risk versus reward scenario that I was willing to take, and I had taken the necessary precautions including, writing the commitment document to my wife and psychiatrist. I am confident that I would not be writing this letter to you had I not gone to that workshop eight months ago.

... *"Why was the heart workshop so profound?" asked my psychiatrist.*

"One of the things I learned when I saw that first psychiatrist in my 20s is that the world is not black and white. It was gray. I was so excited that I bought a beautiful watch that was completely gray. I wanted something that would always remind

me of this new found knowledge. I still have the watch."

"What do you mean by black and white?" she asked.

"Well, in school the answers are either right or wrong. The same is true in the streets where I grew up. There was a code, a way of being. You crossed it and suffered the consequences. There was no ambiguity. Things were either good or bad, right or wrong, black or white."

"My concept of 'gray' is the recognition that the world is not black or white. There truly is ambiguity and that it is best to see it and live your life accordingly. I call that 'living in the gray'. To see and experience the world as a spectrum of gray and reject the black or white perspective. Reject the extremes."

"The heart conference teaches you how to open your heart chakra and become heart centered. I learned how to bring my self, or more precisely my emotional state, to a safe place of warmth, strength, and serenity. With an open heart chakra, you can experience life from the perspective of unconditional love. Experiencing an open heart chakra and learning how to experience life with unconditional love is a life-altering skill. With it, you are both able and willing to experience the full spectrum of life from black, through gray to white; not just the gray. You are able to experience everything life has to offer, whether painful or wondrous, because you don't need to protect yourself. With an open heart chakra, you know you can come to your heart center whenever you need too. As a result, your life experiences and memories are not automatically rejected or filtered. Instead, they are experienced in their purest form. Once experienced; you can see how your memories are impacting your life or the life of another. In this way, giving and receiving unconditional love becomes your norm. It does

not mean, however, that you experience life through rose colored glasses. Quite the contrary. You can now see and experience all as it truly is, but without fear."

"Another teaching is that fear is the opposite of unconditional love. At the core of this dichotomy is vulnerability. Fear is the emotion that stops you from being vulnerable while unconditional love is the emotion that allows you to be completely vulnerable with yourself and others. Ultimately, this means that you can't truly experience the full beauty or wonder of unconditional love if you have not also experienced the terrifying fear of being vulnerable to another person. You can't have one without the other. This concept of needing to know something's antithesis extends to everything: Good versus bad; right versus wrong; happy versus sad; anger versus surrender; and black versus white. As one participant at the heart conference said, happy needs sad and sad needs happy; otherwise everything is the same."

"This reminds me of a conversation I had with Genevieve when she was a little one. She wanted to live in Disney World for the rest of her life. She told me that she loved it there because it was the 'funnest place ever'. Being the pragmatist that I am, I told her that she would eventually get bored. The reason why Disney is so much fun is because we come here only for vacation every couple of years. If we lived here all the time, it would not be so special. She did not like my response, and I had no idea that I had given her a pearl of wisdom."

"At the heart conference, I realized that living in the gray spectrum of life is just as limiting and naive as seeing the world as only black and white. In other words, I need to live life through gray, black and white. Not the colors themselves but the full spectrum from one extreme to the other. Each is *beneficial in their own right. Anger, sadness, and fear are not 'bad'. They are very important emotions that serve you in many fantastic ways. They inform you; they protect you; they can motivate you, and they are the means by which you experience life to its fullest. Avoiding pain is not the answer. Pain and fear have a very real purpose in your life."*

"The heart conference was profound because I finally understood this. I had been living a muted life. One with a limited set of colors, tastes and smells. I was living in one zone out of the full spectrum of life."

"I also learned how to open my essence to unconditional love. I don't need to avoid fear, pain, vulnerability, joy, pride, or any other emotion. I now have the skills to experience the emotions to the fullest because I know how to become heart-centered."

"Life is a rainbow of color!"

noonies

Our response to triggers is both immediate and predictable. We are powerless and often completely unaware of them until they are provoked. But all is not lost. You can empower yourself. You do have a choice, and sometimes, the hand of God will intervene.

... Early in my career, I was an IT consultant conducting training sessions and running workshops where I helped teams build their deliverables through facilitation sessions. I always traveled with at least one other consultant. I was single and on the road about 85% of the time shuttling between home and various North American cities. I enjoyed the independence and experiences. More often than not, my consulting partner was a woman who was about 15 years my senior. Her real name is Mary and she saw the world in an extraordinarily unique way. I cherished our discussions about her philosophical views on life.

One of the things we often talked about was dysfunctional families. Mary believed that people relived their unhealthy birth family relationships in all of their social situations including friendships; marriage; work; clubs; organizations; everything. She believed that we have no choice but to repeat those unhealthy relationships until we figure out how to resolve them and heal.

Whenever I was having difficulty with someone, Mary would ask me to identify who that person represented in my birth family. To my surprise, I could make a connection, and the issue became apparent to me. The key to figuring this out was something she called a 'noony'. (Yes, that is her word for it, and I have never forgotten it. The 'oo' sound in noony is pronounced the same as the 'oo' sound in the words look and book.). She reasoned that identifying, understanding and healing your noonies was the only way to break the repeating cycle and have healthy relationships.

We spent many flights, layovers, meals and car rides discussing noonies. Mary's noonies, my noonies, our co-worker's noonies and our client's noonies. Little did I know that she introduced me to something that I would not fully appreciate for another 25 years. To know my noonies is to know me.

What is a noony? As you know, I believe that the 'story' is much less important than the impact of the story. I have described the impact as having a direct bearing on self-identity and life choices. I have also described how the impact is triggered by an emotional response to something. Recognizing the trigger is the starting point to mindfulness. Mindfulness, in turn, leads to consciousness and choice. Noonies are those things that cause you to have an uncomfortable or unhealthy emotional response to something. Another way to think about noonies is they are mindfulness triggers.

Here is an example of a noony that is sourced from my first memory. If you recall, that event taught me that my need to be comforted is not important to those I love or to those who love me. As a result, I feel very uncomfortable when someone tries to comfort me in any way what so ever. My noony is about needing comfort. Looking back at some of the girlfriends I had before I met my wife, I now understand why I was attracted to them. They were not very compassionate or empathetic people and therefore never triggered that noony.

The Mighty Mouse event provides another example of

a noony. One of my learnings was that I must do difficult things alone. My noony is about needing the help of others. The more difficulty I was in, the less likely I was to ask for help. Whenever I was in a difficult or scary situation, I would look within rather than look to others for help. If I ever considered requesting help or relying on others, I would have an emotional response that caused me to reject or ignore that need.

Both of these noonies still exist in me to some degree. The good news is I am very cognizant of them and consciously work at asking for, and allowing others to comfort or help me.

Here is a memory from when I was about 12 years old. It illustrates my noony about needing the help of others. When you read it, try to imagine how different the events would have been had I been aware of my noony.

... *"No, I don't need a ride. My mother will be here to get me," I replied.*

It was the coldest day of the winter; so cold that the manager of the ice skating rink decided to close the rink after our hockey practice. When I played hockey, I never took a coat with me. I wore only my equipment and hockey jersey because I got hot when I played and did not need to wear anything else.

A couple of the parents asked me if I needed a ride home before they left. I, of course, told them no. I stood there in the parking lot and watched the rink manager turn the lights out. It was 6:00 pm and very dark that night. He came out of the rink, got into his car, asked me if I needed a ride and then drove off. My heart sank. I was cold and very alone.

There was an apartment building with a foyer across the

street. I picked up my stick and hockey bag. I waited by the curb for the traffic to slow and ran to the foyer. The foyer was unheated, and I was freezing.

An elderly man from apartment 102 came out and asked why I was there. I told him, and he asked if I wanted to wait in the apartment and call my mother. I knew I could not get hold of my mother because she was not home; she was with my sister. I said no.

After some period of time, my mother drove into the parking lot. I came running out of the foyer and down the steps tripping over my bag. By the time I made it to the curb, she had driven off. I was devastated.

I went back into the foyer and looked at the mailboxes. They each had an apartment number, a name, and a call button. That elderly man in apartment 102 was named McCarthy. I did not ring his bell.

My only hope now was to walk up the street to the bus stop. I did not have any money on me, and I did not have a key to the house. That was not my biggest fear, however. I figured I could convince the bus driver to let me on for free. I was more concerned about getting jumped by kids in the neighborhood.

I was about halfway up the street when I saw a gang of four kids that were bigger than me walking down the hill toward me. I was scared. I decided that my first move would be to jab my stick in at least one of their eyes and go for the second kid's face. Hopefully, they would run.

I could not cross the street because they would know I was afraid and would chase me.

Also, I cannot run when I am wearing hockey equipment. As they got closer, I held the bag differently so I could easily drop it and two-hand my stick. My hands were cold because I was wearing hockey gloves which have no insulation. To my surprise, it was my brother, cousin and two of our friends. I could not believe it. They were on their way to the rink to go skating. I told them I was freezing, and the rink was closed. They had enough money to pay for my bus fare, and we took turns sharing coats.

My eyes are tearing up as I tell you this story. The story not only illustrates the degree to which I would ignore the helping hand of others, but it also illustrates my decision-making process. My noonies influenced the choices I made that night. I did not accept or ask for help. I suspect that I remembered the name of the elderly gentleman because I must have contemplated ringing his bell, but chose not to. I could have easily frozen to death that night. Would I have made different choices if I did not have the noony about asking for help? I am certain I would have.

This memory illustrates the power and impact of noonies. It also illustrates how our stories reinforce our noonies and therefore, keep us blind. Typically, when I tell this story, I do it in a way that leads the listener to conclude that I was a street-wise, independent, fearless kid. Although it is true that I was a tough city kid, the story is a lie because it is not in service to my essence. The version of the story I have told many times throughout my life hides my true feelings. It makes me blind to the reality of the noony that guided my decision making that evening. Imagine if you can, how I, as a 12-year old, would have responded to the questions of a cop who found me walking the streets that night. 'Why didn't you accept a ride from your friend's parents? Why didn't you try to call your mother or someone else? Why didn't you stay in the foyer where there was some warmth?' 'I don't know,' would be the answer to every one of those questions. The truth is, I did not know because I had no understanding of my noonies, and I would not 'know' until a few years ago.

Understanding how your story hides you from your truth is certainly a necessary step to letting go of your story. But the final step is just as difficult. It requires you to be open, honest and vulnerable with yourself. That means accepting the reality of your failings, fears, and foibles. For instance, I could have told you this story by correctly describing how my noonies influenced those events. I could have then presented very rational arguments supporting the decision-making of a 12-year old boy who's life was full of disappointment and devoid of emotional nurturing. I am certain there is a psychological or sociological profile that I could find to rationalize this and explain my decision making. A profile that would have validated me and my story. A profile that would shield me from my reality. But I did not present that version of the story to you. I did not, because doing so would continue to allow me to hide from myself. It would also shrink my world view, and constrain my options. Dis-empowering me by taking away choice while reinforcing the notion that I am inconsequential.

Prison is punishment because it takes away a person's ability to make choices about how they live their life. Noonies trigger default behaviors that also limit how we live our lives. They are like shackles that take away our life choices. The good news is, handcuffs can be opened with a key, and you have the key to every one of your noonies.

Combining noonies with my learnings from the heart workshop, I now know that the solution is not to banish my noonies from my life. Instead, I must honor them and take them into my essence because they help define me. I must be cognizant of when they occur so that I can choose how to live that moment. My choice may turn out to be consistent with the noony, or it could be different. The point is, I would have a choice in how I lived that moment rather than being blind and controlled by my automatic, default behaviors. Having a choice is very empowering.

As you become aware of your noonies you most likely will become overwhelmed by them. It is OK. Acknowledge the wonder of you for having found a noony and accept that it is yours. You will probably have to experience the noony many times before it will begin to make sense to you.

Finally, I am not a devoutly religious man. Even though I am a Catholic; I rarely attend Mass or go to confession. But I do believe in God. My brother, cousin, and friends were there at the exact moment I needed them most. I am certain, that was an act of divine intervention; my brother and his friends had never taken the bus to the skating rink before that night, or since. Maybe, this was the event that allowed me to believe in the helping hand of God.

fear-less-hope-less-fear

We must rediscover the distinction between hope and expectation.

    Ivan Illich

... "Tony, I am not like you, I need to see a light at the end of the tunnel."

"I am sorry, but I don't need to see it," I said. "I take things as they come and then deal with it. I just don't need hope. I am much more optimistic than you realize."

My wife looked at me incredulously, "How can you say that you are optimistic when you can never tell me things will be OK."

"Babe, I have faith in myself. I know, in the end, I will survive."

"There is more to life than just survival," she said.

I was trying to explain to her what I meant by 'hope less'. I was not hopeless, but I was without hope – hope less. I would not allow myself to have hope. That is the only way I knew how to explain it. I was not doing a very good job describing why I don't need to have hope.

That was my first clue.

... My sister laughed and said, "I'm not holding out any hope

for that to happen."

I replied, "Joseph and I feel the same way, Cathy."

"I am not surprised Tony. We have had so many disappointments in our lives that we won't allow ourselves to be set up for more."

My sister began to recount some of the disappointments we've had during our childhood.

"Wow Cathy, I thought I was the only one who was without hope. It is good to know I am not alone."

That was my second clue.

My third clue came from Margaret J. Wheatley, 'From Hope to Hopelessness' 2002.

'... recall the Buddhist teaching that hopelessness is not the opposite of hope. Fear is. Hope and fear are inescapable partners. Anytime we hope for a certain outcome and work hard to make it a happen, and then we also introduce fear -- fear of failing, fear of loss. Hopelessness is free of fear and thus can feel quite liberating.'

The bottom line is I was afraid to have hope. I was avoiding fear and in the process, living a gray life. This noony is still a very difficult one for me. I have found; however, that I have more hope today than ever before. Hope in the little things of life.

I have always had a deep belief in my ability to pull through any crisis: I know I will survive. Ultimately I have deep faith in myself and little faith beyond my span of control. The thing that is different is that I am now able to allow myself to hope and wish for things that I have no control over. I believe this change occurred when I learned how to open my heart chakra.

There is one additional component to this notion of being without hope that I must mention. It is derived from my intellectualization side. I dislike some of the music my son listens to because the messages are about being a victim. I have told him on many occasions that people who think of themselves as victims will always be victims. It is dis-empowering, and it is self-fulfilling.

I believe that everything that is, must first be conceived in your mind. If you are only able to see yourself as a victim, then you will never become anything but a victim. In this same way, if I am unable to imagine hope, then I will never have any hope. The other thing I dislike about the cult of victim-hood is that it is based on the belief that you are either a victim or the victimizer. It promotes black and white thinking.

Given all of these clues, it is clear that living without hope is a contradiction. How can I continue to live my life without hope? It does not make sense. My wife is ultimately right, 'there is more to life than just survival'.

Finally, I think this is the first time that I learned something from an emotional perspective and then worked it to my intellectual side. In this case, I knew hope during the heart workshop as an emotional entity. Then I attempted to make it a part of my normal thought processes as well. Admittedly, I have a tough time with it. I am, however, committed, and will continue to work at becoming more hopeful.

a framework

I have mentioned my essence a couple of times in this letter but have not yet fully described it. Earlier, I said it is the only place where I can be hurt. I have also described it as an egg located in the center of my chest. Here is another description: My essence is the true, fundamental, unfiltered, and vulnerable me.

I recognize that the description of my essence above is still wanting. I need a framework and more formal terminology to provide you with a better, more complete definition. Please keep in mind that I have no formal training in psychology. What little I do know, I stumbled upon as a result of the journey I have been on for these many years.

Recently I was introduced to the teachings of Carl Jung. My understanding of things seem to align with his teachings and, therefore, believe it is a good foundation for explaining my essence. I will use the basics of Jungian psychology as the framework for describing my essence. Remember, the following is my current understanding of a small piece of his work, and I am a novice.

Jung teaches:

1. People have an innate need to become separate, unique individuals with personalities that are 'distinct from the general, collective psychology'. The purpose of this need is to develop an individual personality that is both differentiated from others and is whole or indivisible from itself. 'Individuation' is the term Jung uses to describe

the process of developing a personality that is both differentiated and indivisible. My personal interpretation of this concept is best illustrated when a child first understands the word 'me'.

Jung also believes that there are two phases of individuation. The first is about establishing one's self in the world. For many, that is a lifetime endeavor. The second phase requires the integration of the conscious and unconscious mind[1]. It is about moving toward awareness, integration, and wholeness. For those who can move to this phase, it usually occurs in the second half of life.

The process of individuation is not to be confused with individualism. Individualism is an Ego-driven world view that fosters selfishness and lack of concern for others. Individuation is very much the opposite of individualism in that it promotes relationship without co-dependence.

2. Jung uses the term 'Self' to describe the totality of one's mind, soul, and spirit. Self is the psyche as separate and distinct from the physical body, and it includes both the conscious and unconscious mind.

3. The 'Ego' is that part of one's Self or psyche that is conscious. As such, the Ego has access to memories that are not repressed at a particular moment in time. The notion of a particular point in time is important because our memories,

---

1   http://jungiancenter.org/essay/components-individuation-1-what-individuation

thoughts, intuitions, feelings, and sensations are not forever resident in our conscious mind. They float between the conscious and the unconscious as part of the individuation process.

The Ego holds and organizes our thoughts, feelings, intuitions, and sensations. It allows one's Self to be aware of our own existence. Our personal identity or our self-identity is defined and managed by the Ego. The Ego holds one's personality, and it stands at the junction between two or more individuals. That junction point is where we create and maintain a relationship with other human beings.

4. The 'Unconscious' is that part of one's Self or psyche that is unknown to the Ego at a particular moment in time. Our thoughts, intuitions, feelings, and sensations, are never lost. They reside in our unconscious mind and come into and out of consciousness as part of the individuation process.

The Ego and the Unconscious are further partitioned as follows:

1. That part of the Ego that is known to others is called the 'Persona'. An individual has many Personae such as father, son, engineer, caregiver, prankster, etc. The Persona is often described as the Ego's public relations person.

2. That part of the Unconscious that is the opposite of one's Persona is referred to as the 'Shadow'. Shadows are the repressed traits or characteristics that we do not want to know about ourselves.

They are the traits we deny and consider them to be evil, inferior or unacceptable. As such, we disown our Shadows because they are in conflict with our self-identity or Persona(s). Frequently the traits, which we find abhorrent in others, are, in fact, our Shadows. Some Shadows are defined by social norms, others are not.

Noonies and Shadows are often coupled. As you know, one of my noonies is about needing the help of others. I am never needy and don't respect people who are. Being needy is one of my Shadow traits. Here is a little hint to help you along your journey. Look for your Shadows and you will find your Noonies. Feel your noonies and you will know when to be mindful.

self-love empowers connectedness

This letter is about my personal process of individuation. I am in the second phase of that process, and I use the term 'journey' to describe that process in totality. The interesting thing is that I did not know that until I just wrote it. This letter is indeed a gift to me because I am able to reflect upon my journey and connect things that I have not yet understood.

My warehouse is my Unconscious Self. Most of the memories, thoughts, feelings, intuitions, and sensations in my warehouse are my disowned Shadow stuff; but not all. Some of the things in the warehouse are simply there because I stifled anything that triggered a strong reaction in me. As I mentioned previously, my ability to push things into my unconscious mind, i.e. my warehouse, is an instantaneous and automatic action.

Jung's notion of Self is the closest thing to what I call my essence. My definition of essence; however, is limited to that part of Self that is under or protected by my Personae. As such, my essence is the inner core of me, not my external interface as presented through my Personae. I am not rejecting my Personae; they are indeed part of me, but they are not the defining part.

As you know, I visualize my essence as an egg located in the center of my chest. Like all eggs, it is surrounded by a hard shell. Previously I described that shell as being impenetrable and made of stone. Today, the shell is only partially made of stone. The remainder of the shell is glass: many faceted pieces of glass. Glass that is also unbreakable. Since the goal of my journey is individuation,

I will know that I have completed my journey when my shell is made completely of glass. At that point, my shell will no longer hide my essence.

Each piece of faceted glass is a different shape, size, and color; like an exquisite stained glass window or a beautiful Tiffany lampshade. In my mind's eye, my essence is beginning to look like a Tiffany glass egg that radiates with a luminous energy passing through each piece of colored glass.

The lead came that frames each piece of glass is forged from the scars accumulated from a lifetime of experience; both good and bad. Earlier, in the first few pages, I mentioned my failings, fears, and foibles. They are the source of these scars.

The lead came, like my scars, are not to be ignored or shunned. They actually can't be ignored because they are a beautiful and intrinsic part of me. They are fundamental to the strength and integrity of my essence in the same way the lead came are fundamental to the strength and integrity of stained glass. They make the Tiffany piece and my essence multidimensional, interesting, and unique.

Each piece of faceted glass was formed from one of my labeled warehouse boxes. The glass is not the content of the box. Rather, it is the learning that resulted from the process of labeling the box. The light and energy that comes into my egg through the glass are not changed by the shape or color of the glass. Instead, the glass is like the lens of a super decoder spy-ring that can see the energy and light as it truly is. The life experiences that form each piece of glass make the energy and light both readable and understandable. That is why I can now see what was previously hidden and love what I once feared.

The glass allows energy and light to pass through it. Light and energy shared between me and the people with whom I am in relationship. But the sharing of energy and the concept of being in relationship is not limited to people. It includes any relationship I have with everything there is. Animals, art, literature, vegetation, automobiles, etc. Close your eyes for a moment and think back to your childhood. That time when you first marveled at something in nature. Something like a spider web. Can you remember a time like that? A time when nothing else mattered, and you were lost in the moment. Can you see the silk fibers glisten from moisture or sway with the wind? Bring yourself back to that point of wonder. That is when you allowed the energy of nature to enter your essence. You were in pure, unfiltered relationship with mother earth.

Another example is your first kiss or the first time you held hands with someone you loved. Certainly there was the sexual energy you were experiencing for the first time, but there was also the wonder of connection with another human being. Try to remove the sexual energy from the memory and feel the connectedness. You were in pure, unfiltered relationship at that moment.

The energy and light are free to enrich me and enrich those with whom I am in contact. That is the treasure that I have found. That is the treasure I want to share with you. The treasure is to be simply with unconditional love and without fear in relationship with others as well as with yourself. The treasure includes the knowledge that it is all possible and also includes the fact that its value grows as more and more people find it.

I need to emphasize the importance of being without fear in relationship with yourself because it is a necessary prerequisite to being in relationship with others. Loving yourself unconditionally is actually the same as being without fear in relationship with yourself. The only way to love yourself unconditionally is to see, know, and accept your essence with all of its failings, fears, and foibles.

At the beginning of this letter, I promised to rewrite a paragraph describing the characteristics of the treasure I have found. The following is that paragraph. I have replaced words like 'treasure' and 'it' with the actual treasure.

I am writing this letter because I want you to have that treasure too. Your essence is limitless, pervasive and unique to you. Its value increases as more and more people are in a relationship with your essence. I want to share this knowledge with you because its value to me will increase when you find your essence, and we can be in a relationship together without fear. Don't rush to find your essence. There is no need to hurry because it is not possible to find it until you are capable of seeing yourself as you truly are. Your essence will come to you only when you are ready to receive it. Finally, do not worry that you will never find your essence: I am certain that you will. It will always be there, waiting for you, and only for you as you pursue your journey.

relationships through vulnerability

I recognize that the description of the treasure in the previous section is a bit esoteric for some. Let me try to explain it from another perspective. Why do we love to watch movies and read books? What is the relationship we have with the characters in the book or movie?

Books and movies give us an intimate glimpse into the lives of other people. What we see of the characters is pure and unfiltered. We can experience their lives in almost every way without the need to be vulnerable to them or anyone else but ourselves. We are anonymous; the characters are not. This anonymity gives us extraordinary freedom, and it allows us to grow and develop through their life experiences in ways we would not have otherwise.

I believe that healthy person-to-person relationships are similar to the relationship we have with the characters in a book. One similarity is that people in a relationship give each other a glimpse into their lives. Often, when there is trust, that glimpse is intimate and significant. In so doing, each person can experience the life of the other. We each benefit from the shared life experience and grow accordingly. However, we are not anonymous like we are as we read a book or watch a movie. This lack of anonymity introduces fear; fear of being seen as we truly are. By the same token, we rarely see the other person in a pure and unfiltered way. Rose colored glasses do exist, and we all have them. Ultimately, the fear of being truly vulnerable triggers the creation of a Persona, which in turn limits our relationships.

As normal, healthy human beings, we need relationships.

Deep, meaningful relationships. This need for relationship is fundamental to our genetic heredity. But relationships require us to be vulnerable. We fear vulnerability because it opens us to pain. In response to the vulnerability, we present ourselves through a Persona and see others through filters. We do this to protect our essence from pain. Our relationships are then based on both the Personae and the filters; not on our essence. That means we cannot have deep, meaningful, pure relationships. We are in a 'Catch 22' unless we are willing and able to be vulnerable.

I describe relationships of this type as being based on bidirectional blindness. Fear; fear of being vulnerable, is the cause of bidirectional blindness in relationships. Fear; the opposite of unconditional love, is an extraordinarily strong force that controls many of our behaviors, thoughts, and interpretations. The human mind is unbelievably powerful and creative. Personae and filters are the creation of the human mind. Together, fear and our minds create the false reality in which we live. They form the relationships we have, as well as the relationships we don't have. If our relationships are fear based, then they will be formed around a false reality.

I do not, however, want you to think relationships formed around a false reality are necessarily bad. If both parties are truly unaware, content and committed, then all is well. Ignorance is bliss, and I don't mean that in a derogatory way. For me, however, I would not be content because I am no longer blind.

I suspect you are now yearning for deep meaningful relationships and probably feel very alone. It is OK. Begin by developing a vulnerable relationship with yourself and be patient with those around you. Remember they are blind and cannot see.

essence masking

Close your eyes for a moment and think about the last time you went to the grocery store. Do you remember the cashier? Probably not. If you do remember, what kind of interaction did you have with the cashier? Was it meaningful? What Persona did you present? What filters did you apply? How about the last time you went to the emergency room or the doctor's office? Think about the interaction you had with the nurse. Compare it with the relationship you had with the doctor. What Persona and filters did you apply? What Persona did they present to you?

What about your youngest cousin, your spouse, an alcoholic uncle, oldest child, mother, men, women, rabbis, even your pets. We all present a Persona in each of these relationships. It is an automatic response, and we are often not even aware that we have triggered them.

Think back to that cashier. What beauty resides within that person that you never got to see? If the cashier were older, for instance, they could have shared a gem of wisdom or an acknowledgment of you based on a cherished memory they have. If the cashier were a teenager, it could have been their wonder of life or the excitement they exude when they catch a glimpse of the other cashier they have a crush on. Do you wish you had that moment with the cashier to live over again? Do you wish you could have shared the real you, and the cashier could have been himself as well?

How do relationships built upon bidirectional blindness work? These relationships depend upon the Personae and the filters through which we see the world. The relationship works when the filter through which I see you, matches or is harmonious with, the Persona you present to me. My Persona must also be compatible with the filter through which you see me. The reverse is also true. When the filters and Personae are not compatible, the relationship fails.

In either case, success or failure, the relationship has nothing to do with who we truly are because it is based on our Personae and filters; not on our essence. Our essence is not shared between us. It is hidden in the dark, unseen, unheard and inconsequential.

The treasure that I have found is the ability to have relationships with one's self as well as with others that are pure and complete. Relationships where everyone's essence is seen and heard with equality and unconditional love. Relationships shared without fear. Relationships where your essence and the essence of the other person are cherished and not inconsequential.

This treasure allows me to be in relationships of all types. I will not fear vulnerability, nor will the other person who is in a relationship with me. There will be no need to filter, and the energy we share will be pure and unconditional. I will be me, and they will be them. Separate, distinct, whole, equal and free.

I need to state the last two sentences again: I will be me, and they will be them. Separate, distinct, whole, equal and free. I also need to say that there is not, and should not, be any expectation of the other person to be in the same depth of relationship with me. My relationship with that other person is based on the beauty of who they are at this moment in time. I do not expect or require them to change.

truth from any angle

I was very lucky with my first job out of college. I worked for two very senior managers at one of the largest defense contractors in the United States. They gave me all sorts of opportunities and mentored me along the way.

... *"Hey Rico, I can't find a good solution."*

"Sit down Tony. Have you flipped the problem upside down?" *he asked.*

"How do I flip the problem upside down and why would I want to do that?" I thought.

"Have you turned it inside out?"

I clearly was confused and said, "I don't understand what you mean, Rico."

Rico had a look on his face that reminded me of Yoda, the Jedi Master of Star Wars. He then said, "Looking at the problem from the inside out; is not the same as looking at the problem only from the outside; or only from the inside?"

It seems Rico introduced me to mindfulness without ever realizing it. I find myself tearing up again. I have obviously forgotten the gifts Rico, and Gaetano gave me so many years ago. I guess I need to tag this memory too.

What if I looked at the treasure from a different perspective? Would the treasure still be of value?

Well, let's presume I had been born into the opposite

life circumstance. A life experience without any trials tribulations, pain or fear. Literally, the ideal world. In this ideal environment, I would still have my essence because having a Self is part of being a normal, healthy person. It is also reasonable for me to visualize my essence as an egg. However, that egg would either not have a shell or it would have a shell of pristine, clear glass that allowed light and energy to pass in and out of it, unhindered. The glass would have to be pristine and clear because I would not have needed to develop a means for protecting my essence from fear or pain. In other words, I would not have had any difficult life experiences that I needed to shove into my warehouse. For that matter, I would not even have a warehouse. Instead, all of my memories would be instantaneously available. There would be no alteration of light or energy as it passed into my core because the glass is not faceted, shaped or colored. Instead, it is smooth and as clear as the air itself. In addition, the light and energy I generate would be pure and unfiltered.

If I were born into this ideal family circumstance, then my mother, father, and siblings would all have the same essence. Their essence would not need a shell. By extension, my aunts, uncles, cousins, in-laws and friends would also be living in this ideal world. They would also have the same essence and energy. We would all be living in Nirvana, the state of perfect happiness and peace.

A common description of Nirvana is that it is the state of perfect happiness and peace where there is a release from all forms of suffering. The last half of that description is key in that suffering[2] must have existed, and been known, for it to have been released. This concept is further

---

2   http://www.merriam-webster.com/dictionary/nirvana

emphasized by the fact that the word Nirvana also means 'to extinguish'.

When my young daughter asked if we could live in Disney World forever, she knew what it was like living in the real world. She wanted to live in a world where there was only fun: no pain, no illness, and no fear. Disney was her Nirvana. As a child growing up with a chronic illness, she knew about pain and fear and could, therefore, appreciate living in an alternate reality.

In summary, looking at the treasure from an alternative perspective has lead to a Nirvana-like world where there is no need for the treasure. I would be living a life of happiness and peace where there was no suffering. Furthermore, suffering would not have been extinguished because it would have never been known to this ideal world. But here is the problem with this Nirvana-like existence: suffering, pain, and fear are not known by the people who live there. How could they know? They have never experienced it.

Previously I described the importance of experiencing the full spectrum of emotions. I used the colors black, gray and white to illustrate this concept. I also stated that I believed unconditional love is the opposite of fear. Finally, recall Gandhi's 7 Social Sins. They recognize the importance of understanding some thing's antithesis. Living in this ideal world would give someone the gift of not experiencing pain, suffering and fear. But it would also prohibit them from experiencing unconditional love because love radiates in the face of fear, suffering and pain. A profound conclusion that leads me to ask: how does this Nirvana state of being, differ from my previous state of 'living in the gray'?

It does not. I don't believe there is a qualitative difference between 'living in the gray' and living in Nirvana because living in either state means you are only aware of a small piece of the full spectrum of life. A Nirvana-like world exists at one of the extremes without any knowledge of the remainder of the spectrum while 'living in the gray' has no knowledge of either of the extremes. Rico taught me to look at problems from many perspectives before finalizing my conclusions. For me, this alternative thought experiment confirms the validity of the treasure. I hope it does for you as well.

Finally, as I have traveled my journey, I could not help but see how I have shaped my children. I also saw how my mother shaped me. In both cases I was initially distraught. Today, however, I am very thankful that my mother gave me the gifts that she did because I would not be the man I am. I also know that my mother had no choice but to shape me as she did. Just like you have had no choice but to shape your children. You see, my mother was blind and could not see beyond her limited sphere of possibility. She could not see or experience the full spectrum of life which I now know is critical to understanding, fulfillment and well-being. But she gave me the anchor, she gave me half the key and set me on my journey to find the other half. For that I am grateful. For my children I am excited.

There is one other thing that I must mention and it may be difficult to understand. My children possess many of my traits including some of my Shadows. I have desperately wanted to erase those shadow traits from them but now I know it is their journey to travel. I also now realize my children have given me a beautiful gift by holding these shadows present for me. The best gift I can give them is to acknowledge and accept those traits in me and in them.

mindful choice

I believe that health and time are the two most valuable resources we have. I don't want to spend any more of my time or energy in ways that do not make my life more fulfilling and healthier. That is why I only want to have relationships where I can be me, and you can be you: separate, distinct, whole, equal and free. I don't want to be in any relationship where that is not possible. That includes the relationship I have with myself. This is an important concept to understand, and I am making the choice consciously. I am choosing to make my life and my relationships more fulfilling. That is why I am demanding change in the way I think, see and experience the world. This change is about me; not others. It is directed at me, and no one else. And it is possible only because I have a choice in the way I live my life.

How much choice do you have in your life? I am not talking about choosing your clothes or what to eat. I am also not asking about those times when you are not able to do something because you have a responsibility of some sort. For instance, when your child is sick or needs a bath or when work demands your time. My question about choice is much more fundamental. It is about how you choose to live each and every moment of your life. Take this very moment for instance. The moment that passes as you read these words. It is my hope that this moment is of value to you: not your Persona, but your essence.

Think back to the cashier we discussed earlier. There was a moment of interaction when your automatic Persona took over. That automatic response was not by your choice. You were ultimately unconscious during that time. How many moments in your life are spent in an automatic, unconscious state?

It is important to note that becoming more conscious or mindful does not mean that your automatic response or Persona is wrong. It may, in fact, be the best thing for you, at that point in time. The difference is that being mindful gives you the opportunity to make the choice of how you want to be at that moment. Even if the choice is the same as it would have been with your automatic response. Making the choice is an act of empowerment and insight. It is also a prerequisite to finding your puzzle pieces.

Let me emphasize that I am not suggesting the elimination of your Personae. Not at all. Your Personae serve and protect you. The goal is to recognize when a Persona interferes with you as you experience a moment or a relationship. Becoming mindful is a critical prerequisite to your ability to detect when an automatic response has triggered a Persona. Recognizing the trigger is the key to having a choice. You can choose how you want to experience that moment or that relationship. Your choices are:

- Ignore the moment and simply respond to it in an automatic, default way
- Keep the default Persona and filter(s)
- Keep the default Persona but change the filter(s)
- Change the Persona and filter

I know that it is not as simple as it sounds. Becoming mindful takes practice. That is why I believe it is important to have faith in yourself and the power of your mind. You should also know that I am not always able to do this. If I am lucky, I do it 50% of the time. I wish I could do it more, but I am not yet able. I get triggered when I am interacting with some folks, and my automatic behaviors take over. I am still on my journey and have far to travel. But I have been lucky enough to experience relationships where my essence can flourish. Becoming mindful is both possible and beneficial to you and to all the people you are interacting with.

There are two ways to know when you are mindful when you are with people. One way is when you are acutely aware of the person you are in a relationship with at that moment in time. The second is that you are at peace as you interact with the other person. More importantly, you know that you are at peace.

Being at peace does not mean that the interaction you are having is necessarily blissful or devoid of stress. You can be in conflict with the other person and, in peace at the same time. Being in peace while in conflict means your defense mechanisms are not ruling you. You know it is 'OK' to be in conflict, and you are comfortable with the interaction. I recognize that this notion of being in peace and, in conflict at the same time sounds like crazy new-age speak, but trust me, it is possible when your heart chakra is open.

How does one become mindful? How do you recognize that you are not and instead are in an automatic response mode? How do you interrupt yourself and become conscious of the moment? The following six-step process is what I have done to develop the skill of being mindful. Unfortunately, I do not do this all the time. I sometimes get overwhelmed or simply forget. The other thing to note is that these steps happen instantaneously when you become adept at them. These steps happen so fast that you don't know you are doing them.

When you first attempt to do these steps, do not try to do all six of the steps. Just practice the first step again and again. Then, practice the first and second step in the sequence. When you have mastered the first two steps, add the third. Repeat this process until you have practiced all six steps, one after the other. The process is:

1. Become adept at recognizing that you are in a relationship with someone. For instance, every time you interact with a cashier, simply recognize that is what you are doing. You don't have to do anything special. Just acknowledge the fact that you are in a relationship with him at that very moment. You will probably make eye contact and smile.

2. Notice what is going on around you. Notice what the cashier is doing. Take note of what the cashier is wearing and what facial expression they have. Notice any smells or sounds. Simply notice stuff.

3. Identify how you feel or what you are thinking. Are you angry because the cashier is making mistakes, and you think the cashier is an idiot? Are you amazed at the bar code scanner technology? Or maybe you are worried that the people behind you are getting frustrated because you are taking too long looking for change.

4. Determine which of your many Personae you are presenting to the cashier? What filters are obscuring your view of the cashier i.e. how are you experiencing her? You may find that you have Personae you never knew existed. Try very hard to be honest and objective with yourself during

this step. This is not an easy step.

5. Decide if you want to keep the current Persona and filter or change it. Make this a conscious decision but do not yet act on it.

6. Make the decision in step 5 happen.

additive moments

Each and every moment of your life matters; it really does.

... "Why do you spend all that money to go to Disney World when there are so many other places you can go?" asked a co-worker who dislikes Disney because 'nothing there is real'.

I said, "Because it is the only place I know where you will find a tired, hot and hungry New Yorker, in a crowd of people with a smile on his face."

My co-worker did not understand my response. He did not understand the value of authentic smiles. He did not understand the possibility that the Disney experience can be about the joy and the freedom to experience life through the eyes of children. He did not know that it is the only place in the world where I can be with that little inconsequential boy that is me. The surprising thing is that I did not understand that either, until now, as I wrote it.

My response to my co-worker was a recollection of a vivid memory. An interaction between a parent and their child that I have seen many times at Disney. The first time was with a boy about ten years old and his father who had a very strong Brooklyn accent and the calloused, dirty hands of an auto mechanic. I don't even remember what the father and son were doing at the time. My guess is that we were on the monorail, but I am not certain. One of the things I remember clearly; however, is the smile that was on the father's face when his son said something to him. For that one brief moment, that father was in a relationship with himself and his boy in a way that neither he nor his son often get to share. The real joy; however, occurred when I saw the face of the 10-year-old boy after he saw his father's smile. That moment was additive to me. That moment was also additive to the boy, and I hope, to his dad as well.

finding your stranger

I have a friend who would often tell me she was afraid to start a journey of her own; even though she understood its potential and yearned for its benefits. I was chatting with her about something innocuous when her eyes welled up with tears.

... "OMFG!" she blurted. "What if I don't like what I find? What if I don't recognize the person that is hidden inside me? Will I still be the center of attention, will people still love me and enjoy my company? I have lived my life without ever seeing me?" She then looked me in the eyes and said, "What if I don't like me?"

I was perplexed because my comment had nothing to do with her or the notion of 'finding the inner you'. I asked what triggered her tears. She said it was my journey.

"Do you understand what just happened to you?" I asked. "Do you realize how big a step forward you just took?"

"No," she said. "All I know is I pictured my inner-self and got very frightened."

I replied with the following explanation, "My journey is about me loving myself so that I am capable of loving others and the world around me. To love oneself you must confront the person you are and accept your failings, fears, and foibles without blame and also without shame. However, before you can do that, you must first realize that there is a 'you' hidden within. Then comes the realization that you may indeed reject the hidden you. Most people can't do that, and you just did. This is a significant point in your self-awareness".

She told me that she just wants to ignore it because it makes her sad.

I asked her if she honestly believed it was possible to keep this thought from recurring. Before she could answer, I told her that I know with certainty that it would pop into her head again and again. I also told her that I am also certain that she has had these thoughts before. The difference, this time, is that it was palpable. It was real and something she could not ignore. I told her that it was frightening because she realized that her inner, hidden self, may indeed be revolting to her. Tears trickled down her cheeks.

"What if I don't recognize me? I am afraid that my inner-self is a stranger."

I asked, "Why do you fear strangers? Everyone you have ever known was once a stranger."

She did not reply.

I then said, "Your inner-self is a stranger because you have never said hello to her." She looked at me incredulously.

"What is the opposite of love?" I asked.

"Hate," she said. "Or maybe anger."

I shook my head no, "Fear is the opposite of love, not hate or anger."

She disagreed and told me that fear has nothing to do with love.

I asked her if she remembered a guy we both knew named Pete. To put it mildly, Pete's character is wanting. He is only driven to fulfill his needs, and he is incapable of acknowledging the needs of others; including his kids.

I asked her if she was afraid of him. She said, "No, absolutely not!"

I asked if she could love him and her answer was the same, "absolutely not."

Before I could ask why, she told me that she did not trust Pete.

We then discussed the concepts of trust and vulnerability. She acknowledged that she could not be vulnerable with anyone that she did not trust, and she also agreed that trust is the basis of love.

"What prohibits you from being vulnerable to people?" I asked.

"I'd be afraid to be vulnerable. Afraid of being ridiculed or shamed or being taken advantage of."

I then asked her if she would ever ridicule, shame or take advantage of her children.

"Oh my God, no!" she said. "I love them and want them to be free with me."

I smiled at her and said, "Now you know why I believe fear is the opposite of love. And that is also why you fear the stranger that is hiding within."

She appeared overwhelmed, so I tried to explain what I meant, "You just said that you love your children and want them to be free enough to be vulnerable with you. I bet the thing that would hurt you the most is if your children were afraid to be vulnerable with you. Isn't that right?" I asked. "That means vulnerability is a fundamental part of love. Fear is the thing that prohibits people from being vulnerable. In other words, fear is the opposite of love."

She understood even though it was obvious to me that she was wrestling with this different perspective on love. I then asked her if she would be able to love herself if she feared her inner stranger.

"OMG Tony, you just made it worse."

I shook my head no and replied, "I did not make it worse. I made it very clear. I asked if it was possible to love yourself if you don't know who you are."

I proceeded, "We have all read books that say the key to happiness is to love yourself. What the hell does that really mean? How do you love yourself when you don't even know the inner you? How do you love yourself when you don't know what is prohibiting you from loving yourself in the first place?"

I looked at her and said, "The big thing you just experienced; the big realization you just had; is that you now know what is prohibiting you from loving yourself. That is a gift. That is a major milestone."

"No, I don't Tony. I don't know anything. All I know is that I am afraid, and I don't want to be."

"You just said it," I replied. "It is your fear of confronting the real you. You fear being vulnerable to yourself. You fear your essence. You believe your personae are so far removed from who you really are that you won't be able to find yourself. And to make matters worse, you fear finding the inner you because you realize that she has been hidden away for so long you won't recognize her as you. I know with certainty that you will cherish and protect her just as you have done with your children."

"When I started my journey, I had no clue. All I knew was that I needed to include emotion into my life and that there was a little boy in me that wanted to be seen; he wanted to be consequential. I truly had no idea that I was detached from him. Eventually I realized that the only way I could reconnect was by finding him and loving him unconditionally."

"Close your eyes, take a deep breath and wrap your arms around that beautiful, fragile, frightened, flawed stranger within. Give that little girl the love she has never had."

Everyone's journey starts differently yet begins the same.

discover your essence

My journey has been insightful, beautiful, and at times painful. Earlier, I said 'I am trying to open and allow the pain into my essence.' Why would I pursue pain as a part of my journey? Why do I want to allow the fear, shame and dread within?

I have come to learn that healing occurs when the memories and their associated feelings, become an intrinsic part of me. Only, when I can merge and accept the memory, will its impact no longer limit me like prison shackles. Once accepted, the memory and its feelings are free to float into and out of my essence; informing me about me. That is when I become free to experience the world without the fear associated with painful memories. This process of entwining the memory into the beautiful tapestry that is me is quite empowering.

I have also found that this melding process has made me stronger and more confident. I know, without a doubt, who I am. I know that I can confront new situations without the limitations and automatic behaviors of the past. Ultimately, I know that I have choice in my life. I can choose how I want to experience each and every moment of my life. I am a more powerful, yet more humble being capable of giving and receiving unconditional love. I also know that this is not something that only I can do. You can do it too.

I must interject a comment at this point. Trust me when I tell you that years ago, had I read or heard these words from another source, my eyes would have rolled around in disdain. I'd say to myself, who cares, and this guy is one of those crazy people that preys on the weak. I still have disdain for people who prey on others. But my journey has given me a new perspective on life. I now see the world, and relationship with others differently.

I want for you to start a journey of your own. I want you to believe you can. I want you to have faith in yourself. Have faith in your ability to both protect and stretch yourself. I also want you to know that you and you alone must travel it because it is an intimate, individual endeavor. Alone does not mean without the participation of others. Many people have already come into your life and have contributed to your learnings. New people will appear. Some will take your hand and guide you along the way. Accept their help and acknowledge their gifts to you. But, you must remember that no one can do it for you. No one but you knows the path you must follow. There is no magic elixir or some super special secret known only by a select few. You already know everything you need to know.

At times, your journey will be lonely, scary, and painful. But the peace and serenity you will feel as you heal easily outweighs the pain and fear. Finally, beware of those who tell you that you need them to travel your journey. They are concerned only about themselves.

I am grateful to the many people who helped me along the way. Some people have helped me in ways they will never know. Others wanted to help me, and did while some did not. I sought guidance from a small handful of people in addition to my psychiatrist. But in the end, I took each step alone. It is the only way.

Have faith in yourself. Have faith in the power of your mind and the wisdom of your heart. Be patient and let things happen. Be aware and become mindful. See what you have not seen, and feel what you have not felt. You can undertake your journey, and I know you will succeed.

With each day, you will learn more and more about yourself. Accept that it will take time; lots of time. Cherish the journey. But don't forget, learning is a building process. You need a base before you can build the foundation, and you need the foundation before you can build the floor. As I mentioned earlier, you must learn to count before you can add. This letter is an introduction to the concept of memory addition. The taking of seemingly independent, random memories and combining them together into a greater understanding of one's self. Rest assured that you already know how to count. Otherwise, you would not be reading these words.

faith & love, serenity & grace

I started this letter by describing the moment in time when I found out that I was inconsequential. I then presented bits and pieces of my personal journey toward healing and self-worth. I was motivated to start my journey because my life felt muted, limited, colorless and tasteless. Those feelings were the by-product of having boxed my memories as a coping mechanism for being inconsequential. My life was muted because I built a stone shell around my essence and developed personae to rationalize the corresponding incongruity. I have learned that personae are masks that hide my essence.

I am ending this letter with the recognition that a life restricted to a small set of personae is not the life I want. I have learned that these masks do not change who I am or protect me from pain. Rather, they limit my life experience by hiding me from everything and everyone; including myself. I have also learned that the masks serve a purpose and should not be shunned. The key is being able to recognize which persona, if any, is appropriate for the circumstance. Thus, I have choice and choice is both empowering and necessary for human expression. Without expression, I am hidden and do not exist. If I do not exist, then I am indeed, inconsequential.

I have come to believe that the human mind is extraordinarily powerful. It is capable of many things including self-healing. All you need is the desire to find your true self; the strength to confront your failings, fears, and foibles; the insight to observe objectively, and the patience to let it all happen.

With love,

Me

Made in the USA
San Bernardino, CA
19 October 2017